I0435968

United States
Department of
Agriculture

Forest Service

Northern
Research Station

Resource Bulletin
NRS-74

USDA

Missouri Timber Industry: An Assessment of Timber Product Output and Use

2009

Ronald J. Piva
Thomas B. Treiman

Abstract

In 2009, there were 401 active primary wood-processing mills in Missouri, 12 more mills than in 2006. However, between those years, the number of sawmills that process more than 1 million board feet decreased by 20 mills, and the total volume processed decreased by more than 20 percent. Industrial roundwood harvested decreased by 18 percent, from 125.5 million cubic feet in 2006 to 102.6 million cubic feet in 2009. Of the harvested volume, 95.6 million cubic feet was used by primary wood-processing mills in Missouri and 7.0 million cubic feet was sent to primary wood-processing mills in other states and countries. Saw logs accounted for 90 percent of the total harvest. The harvesting of industrial roundwood produced 71.6 million cubic feet of harvest residues. Primary wood-processing mills generated 1.5 million green tons of mill residues. Five percent of the mill residues generated were not used for other secondary uses.

Cover Photo

Log truck. Photo used with permission of Missouri Department of Conservation.

Contents

INTRODUCTION

Missouri's primary wood products manufacturing industry[1] employs 17,700 workers and has a total value of shipments of $5.9 billion (U.S. Census Bureau 2007). Given the importance of this industry to the economy of Missouri, this bulletin analyzes recent forest industry trends and reports the results of a detailed study of forest industry, industrial roundwood production, and associated primary mill wood and bark residue in 2009. Such detailed information is necessary for intelligent planning and decisionmaking in wood procurement, economic research, forest resources management, and forest industry development.

The last published report of timber product output and use in Missouri was for a 2006 study and is used here as a basis for comparison. When new surveys are completed, errors and omissions from previous surveys are corrected. As a result of our ongoing efforts to improve the survey's efficiency and reliability, changes may have been made to the previous survey's data. All comparisons and analysis in this report are based on the reprocessed data from earlier surveys, which may not match earlier published data. Rows and columns of supporting tables may not sum due to rounding, but data in each table cell are accurately displayed.

Information about the forest land resources of Missouri is available at the Forest Inventory and Analysis Web site at: http://nrs.fs.fed.us/fia/data-tools/state-reports/MO.

The Authors

RONALD J. PIVA, a forester, works for the Forest Inventory and Analysis program at the Northern Research Station in St. Paul, MN. He received a B.S. in forest management from the University of Missouri-Columbia in 1984 and joined the Forest Service in 1987.

THOMAS B. TREIMAN, a natural resource economist, works at the Missouri Department of Conservation's Conservation Research Center, Columbia, MO. He received a Ph.D. in natural resource economics from the University of Wisconsin-Madison.

---

[1]North American Industry Classification System (NAICS) 321–wood product manufacturing, and NAICS 322–paper manufacturing.

STUDY METHODS

This study was a cooperative effort between the Forestry Division of the Missouri Department of Conservation (MDC) and the Forest Inventory and Analysis (FIA) unit at the Northern Research Station (NRS) of the U.S. Forest Service. The FIA program is responsible for providing forest resource statistics for all ownerships across the United States, including timber product outputs.

MDC Forestry Division personnel surveyed all known primary wood-using mills, using questionnaires supplied by NRS, to obtain a 100-percent response rate. The questionnaires were designed to determine the size and composition of the State's primary wood-using industry, its use of roundwood, and its generation and disposition of wood residues. Completed questionnaires were sent to the NRS for processing and analysis. As part of data processing, all industrial roundwood volumes reported on the questionnaires were converted to standard units of measure using regional conversion factors (Table 1). Timber removals by source of material and harvest residues generated during logging were estimated from standard product volumes using factors developed from logging utilization studies previously conducted by the NRS. To provide a complete assessment of Missouri's timber product output, data on the State's industrial roundwood receipts were loaded into a regional timber removals database where they were supplemented with data on out-of-State uses of Missouri roundwood.

Certain terms used in this report—retained, exports, imports, production, and receipts—have specialized meanings and relationships unique to the FIA program that surveys timber product output (TPO) (Fig. 1).

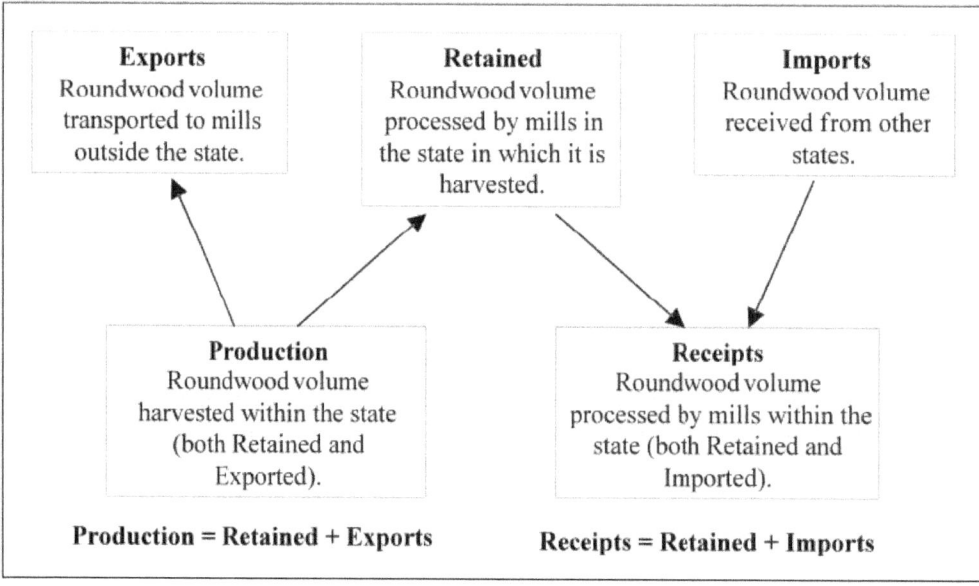

Figure 1.—The movement of industrial roundwood.

Table 1.—Conversion factors from reported unit of measure to standard unit of measure[a]

	Reported unit of measure						
Product (Standard unit of measure)	International ¼-inch rule MBF	Doyle scale MBF	Scribner scale MBF	Green tons	Standard cords	Thousand pieces	Thousand cubic feet
Saw logs and handles							
(MBF International ¼-inch rule)	1	1.38	1.08	0.2174	0.5	--	0.158
Veneer logs and cooperage							
(MBF International ¼-inch rule)	1	1.14	1.04	--	0.5	--	0.158
Pulp and composite products, and industrial fuelwood							
(Standard cords)	--	--	--	0.4167	1	--	0.079
Mine timbers							
(Thousand cubic feet)	--	0.2322	0.1817	--	0.079	6.7	1
Poles							
(Pieces)	20	--	--	4.348	10	1,000	0.0079
Posts							
(Thousand pieces)	0.2	--	--	0.04167	0.1	1	0.79
Cabin logs, excelsior/shavings, and miscellaneous products							
(Thousand cubic feet)	0.158	0.21804	0.17604	0.0329193	0.079	7.9	1

[a] Reported volume times conversion factor = standard volume. For example, a sawmill reports receiving 100 green tons of industrial roundwood; to convert to MBF International ¼-inch rule, 100 X 0.2174 = 21.74 MBF International ¼-inch rule.

PRIMARY TIMBER INDUSTRY IN MISSOURI
Industrial Roundwood

Mill receipts

- Missouri's active primary wood-using industry included 366 sawmills, 9 cooperage mills, 9 post and pole mills, 5 charcoal plants, and 12 mills that produced other miscellaneous products (Table 2, Fig. 2).

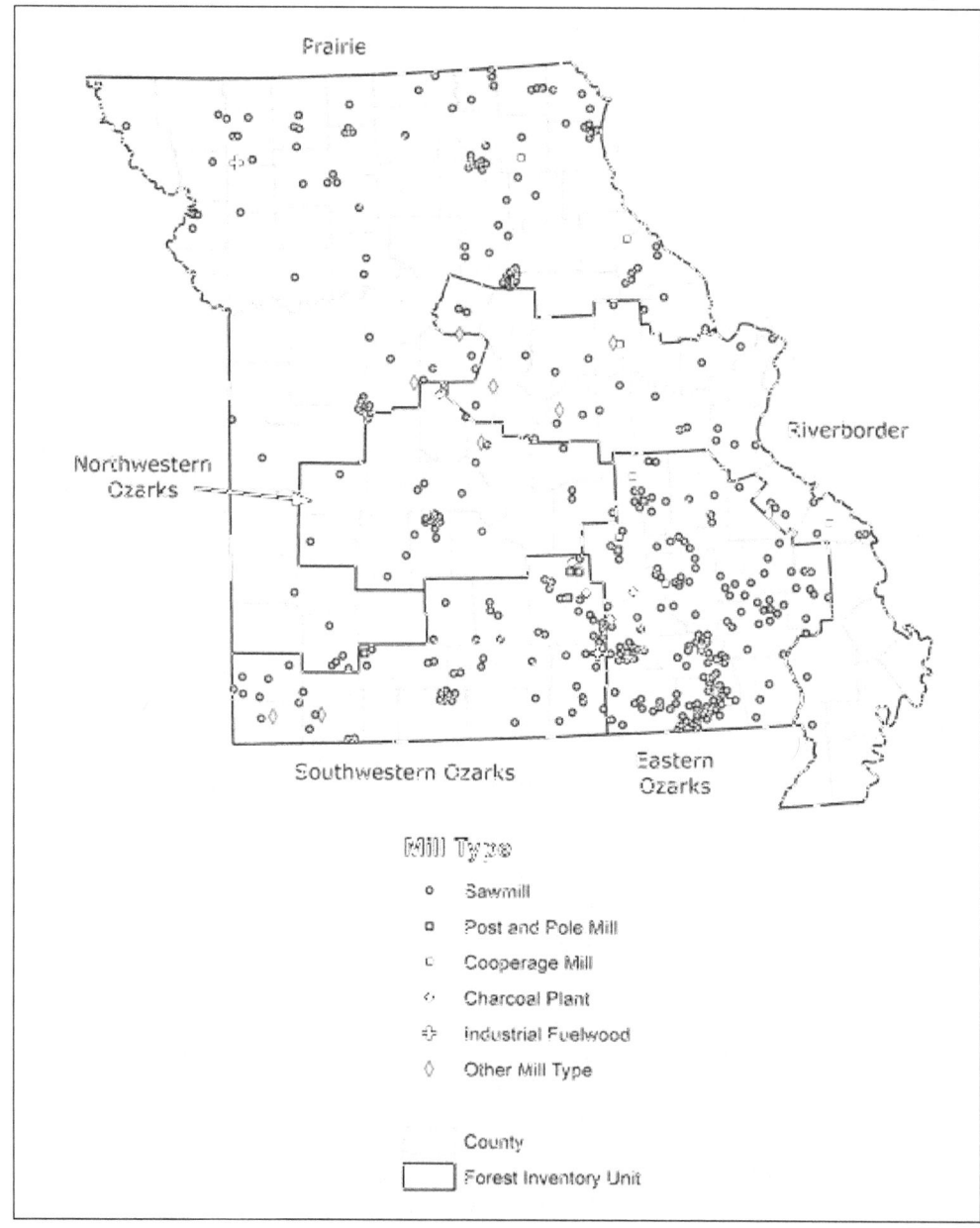

Figure 2.—Missouri Forest Inventory Units and approximate locations of active primary wood-using mills, 2009.

- The total number of sawmills in the State increased from 356 in 2006 to 366 in 2009. However, the number of large sawmills (mills sawing more than 5 million board feet per year) fell from 38 in 2006 to 25 in 2009, and the number of medium sawmills (mills sawing between 1 and 5 million board feet per year) fell from 151 to 144. Many of these mills were still active, but not operating at full capacity.

- All of the other mill types increased in number except for pulp mills, which remained at 1, and handle mills, which fell from 4 in 2006 to 1 in 2009.

- Receipts of industrial roundwood at Missouri primary wood-using mills totaled 102.9 million cubic feet in 2009, a decrease of 21 percent from the 129.7 million cubic feet received in 2006 (Table 3).

- Ninety-three percent of the industrial roundwood processed by Missouri's primary wood-using mills was harvested from forests within the State. Arkansas and Illinois each supplied 2 percent of the industrial roundwood consumed by Missouri mills, with the remainder coming from Indiana, Iowa, Kansas, Kentucky, Nebraska, Ohio, Oklahoma, Tennessee, West Virginia, and Wisconsin (Table 4).

- Ninety-three percent of the industrial roundwood processed by Missouri primary wood-using mills was made up of hardwoods. Red oaks and white oaks combined accounted for 80 percent of the total volume processed. Other important species processed were black walnut, hickories, shortleaf pine, eastern redcedar, and cottonwood.

Industrial roundwood production (harvest)

- Industrial roundwood production decreased by 18 percent, from 125.5 million cubic feet in 2006 to 102.6 million cubic feet in 2009 (Table 5, Fig. 3).

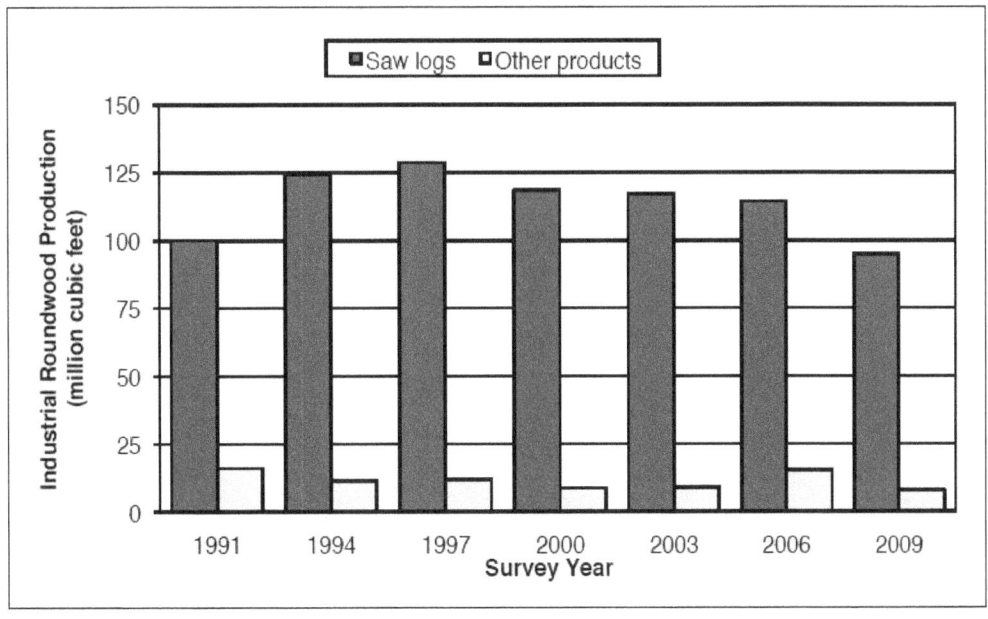

Figure 3.—Industrial roundwood production by product and survey year, Missouri (Hackett et al. 1993, Piva and Jones 1997, Piva et al. 2000, Piva and Treiman 2003, Treiman and Piva 2005, Treiman et al. 2008).

- Ninety-three percent of industrial roundwood harvested in Missouri was retained for processing by primary wood-using mills in the State. Mills in Kentucky and Iowa received 43 and 26 percent, respectively, of Missouri's industrial roundwood exports. (Table 6). Nine percent of Missouri's industrial roundwood exports (predominantly black walnut and white oak) went to other countries.

- The Eastern Ozarks Forest Inventory Unit produced 45.1 million cubic feet of industrial roundwood, 44 percent of total State production, followed by the Southwestern Ozark unit (21.1 million cubic feet, 21 percent of total), the Prairie unit (16.1 million cubic feet, 16 percent of total), the Riverborder unit (11.6 million cubic feet, 11 percent of total), and the Northwestern Ozark unit (8.7 million cubic feet, 8 percent of total).

- The Southwestern Ozark unit, with a 6-percent increase, was the only unit in the State that reported an increase in production of industrial roundwood from 2006 to 2009. Industrial roundwood production decreased by 19 percent in the Eastern Ozark unit between 2006 and 2009, by 22 percent in the Northwestern Ozark unit, by 28 percent in the Prairie unit, and by 31 percent in the Riverborder unit (Fig. 4).

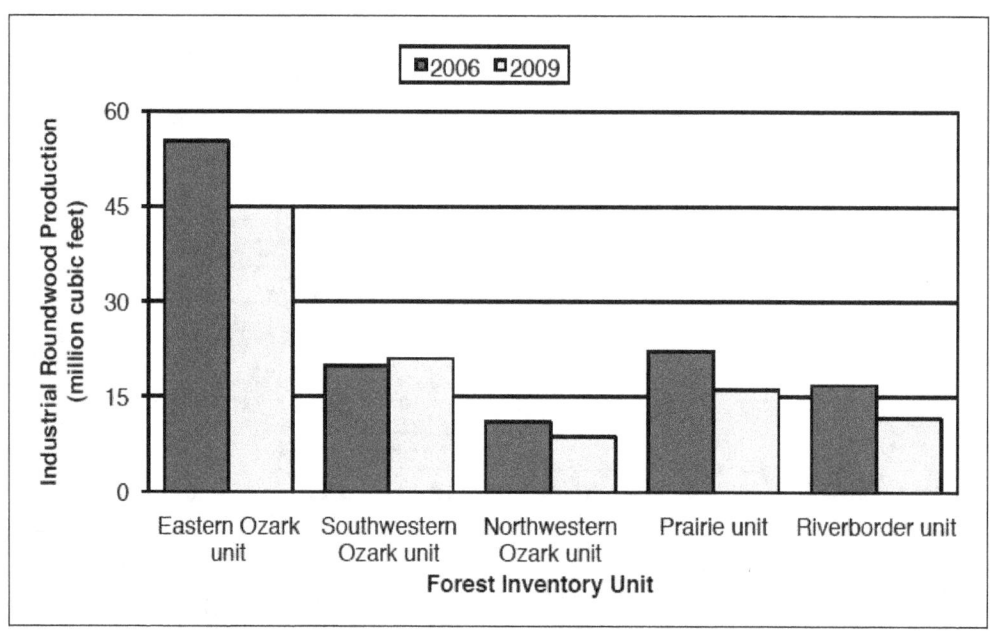

Figure 4.—Industrial roundwood production by Forest Inventory Unit, Missouri, 2006 and 2009.

- Red oaks and white oaks combined accounted for nearly 75 percent of the total industrial roundwood harvested. Black walnut (5 percent), hickory (5 percent), shortleaf pine (4 percent), and eastern redcedar (3 percent) were other major species groups harvested (Table 7, Fig. 5).

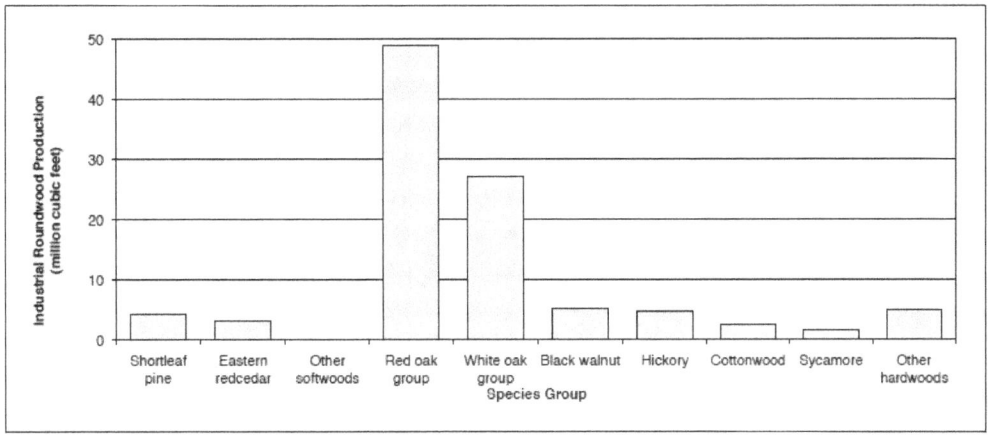

Figure 5.—Industrial roundwood production by species group, Missouri, 2009.

- The production of saw logs accounted for 89 percent of total industrial roundwood production. Pulp and composite products and veneer logs were second in production, accounting for 4 percent and 3 percent of the total volume, respectively (Table 8, Fig. 6).

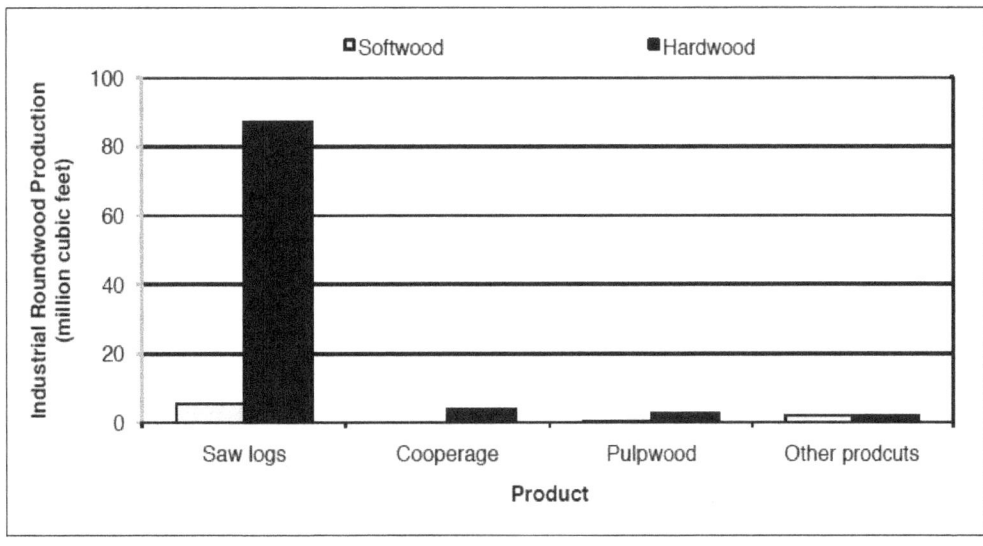

Figure 6.—Industrial roundwood production by product, Missouri, 2009.

Saw Logs

- Receipts at Missouri sawmills totaled 536.8 million board feet in 2009, a decrease of 17 percent from 648.8 million board feet in 2006 (Table 9). Sawmills in the Eastern Ozark unit processed 44 percent (235.7 million board feet) of the State's total saw log receipts.

- Even though the number of total sawmills reported in 2009 increased from 356 mills in 2006 to 366 mills in 2009, the number of mills that processed more than 1 million board feet decreased by 20 mills. Many of these mills were still operating in 2009, but at a lower production capacity, thus moving them to a lower production size category.

- Saw log production decreased by 16 percent between 2006 and 2009, from 618.3 million board feet to 517.7 million board feet.

- Three-quarters of the saw logs produced in Missouri in 2009 were from the red oak or white oak species groups. Other important species groups for saw log production in Missouri were hickory (5 percent of total), black walnut (4 percent of total), shortleaf pine (3 percent of total), and cottonwood (3 percent of total) (Fig. 7).

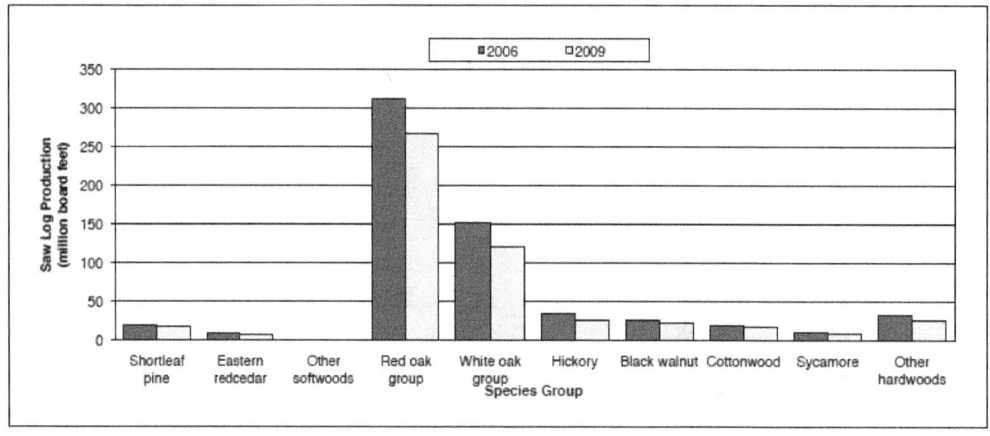

Figure 7.—Saw log production by species group, Missouri, 2006 and 2009.

Other Products

- Cooperage, at 3.8 million cubic feet, was the second most harvested product from Missouri's forests in 2009. Cooperage production fell by 28 percent from 2006 to 2009. Only white oaks are used for cooperage in Missouri.

- Despite having only one pulp mill in the State, pulpwood is the third most harvested product. More than 95 percent of the 3.0 million cubic feet harvested went to mills in other states. See Piva (in prep) for the results of a separate Northern Region pulpwood study conducted for 2009.

- The remaining 3 percent of the industrial roundwood produced in Missouri was sent to cabin log mills, veneer mills, post and pole mills, industrial fuelwood mills, handle mills, charcoal plants, and excelsior/shavings mills.

- Residential fuelwood is not included in this report.

Timber Removals

- During the harvest of industrial roundwood from Missouri's forests in 2009, 102.6 million cubic feet of wood material was used for primary wood products and another 71.6 million cubic feet of wood material was left on the ground as harvest residues (Tables 10 and 13, Fig. 8).

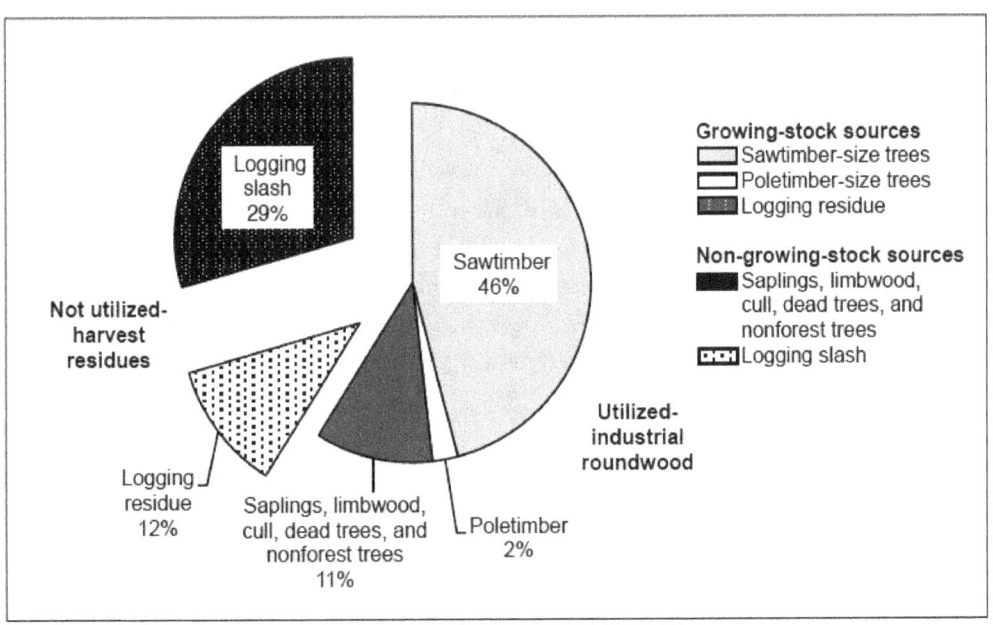

Figure 8.—Distribution of timber removals for industrial roundwood by source of material, Missouri, 2009.

- Growing-stock sources (merchantable material), at 104.3 million cubic feet, were the largest component of removals for industrial roundwood production. Eighty-one percent of the growing stock removed was used for products and 19 percent was left as logging residue. Sawtimber-size trees accounted for 95 percent of the growing-stock volume used for products.

- Non-growing-stock sources of industrial roundwood amounted to 69.8 million cubic feet of wood material removed. Only 27 percent of this material was used for products; the remainder was left on the ground as logging slash. Nearly 70 percent of the non-growing-stock material used for industrial roundwood products came from cull trees. The remainder came from nonforest trees, dead trees, limbwood, and saplings.

- Fifty-five percent of the total growing-stock material removed from Missouri's timberland came from the Eastern Ozark unit, followed by the Southwest Ozark unit with 20 percent, the Prairie unit with 15 percent, the Riverborder unit with 11 percent, and the Northwest Ozark unit with 9 percent (Table 11).

- Nearly 400.0 million board feet was removed from Missouri's sawtimber inventory. The red oak and white oak groups accounted for 75 percent of the total sawtimber volume removed (Table 12).

Harvest Intensity

- Statewide in 2009, FIA reported 34.3 cubic feet of annual net growth of live trees per acre per year on forest land (total annual net growth of live trees divided by forest land area) and 10.5 cubic feet of harvest-related live tree removals per acre per year on forest land (total annual harvest removals of live trees divided by forest land area) (Moser et al. 2010). These are the average net growth and average harvest removals each year from 2005 through 2009.

- Based on this TPO study for Missouri, the current removals for the year 2009 averaged 11.3 cubic feet of total harvest removals per acre of forest land. Seventy-two of Missouri's 114 counties (63 percent) had less than 10.0 cubic feet of harvest removals per acre of forest land. Only five counties had more than 25.0 cubic feet of harvest removals per acre of forest land (Fig. 9). (For reference, a cord of roundwood contains about 80 cubic feet of wood.)

- The Eastern Ozark unit had the greatest harvest intensity: 17.9 cubic feet of wood removals per acre of forest land. The second greatest intensity was in the Southwestern Ozark unit with 12.5 cubic feet of removals per forest land acre, followed by the Prairie unit (8.4 cubic feet/acre), the Riverborder unit (7.9 cubic feet/acre), and the Northwestern Ozark unit (5.7 cubic feet/acre).

- Missouri's net volume of live trees on forest land in 2009 was 20.4 billion cubic feet (Moser et al. 2010). The 174.2 million cubic feet of total wood material removed because of harvesting (Table 10) represents only 0.8 percent of the total live volume of trees on forest land.

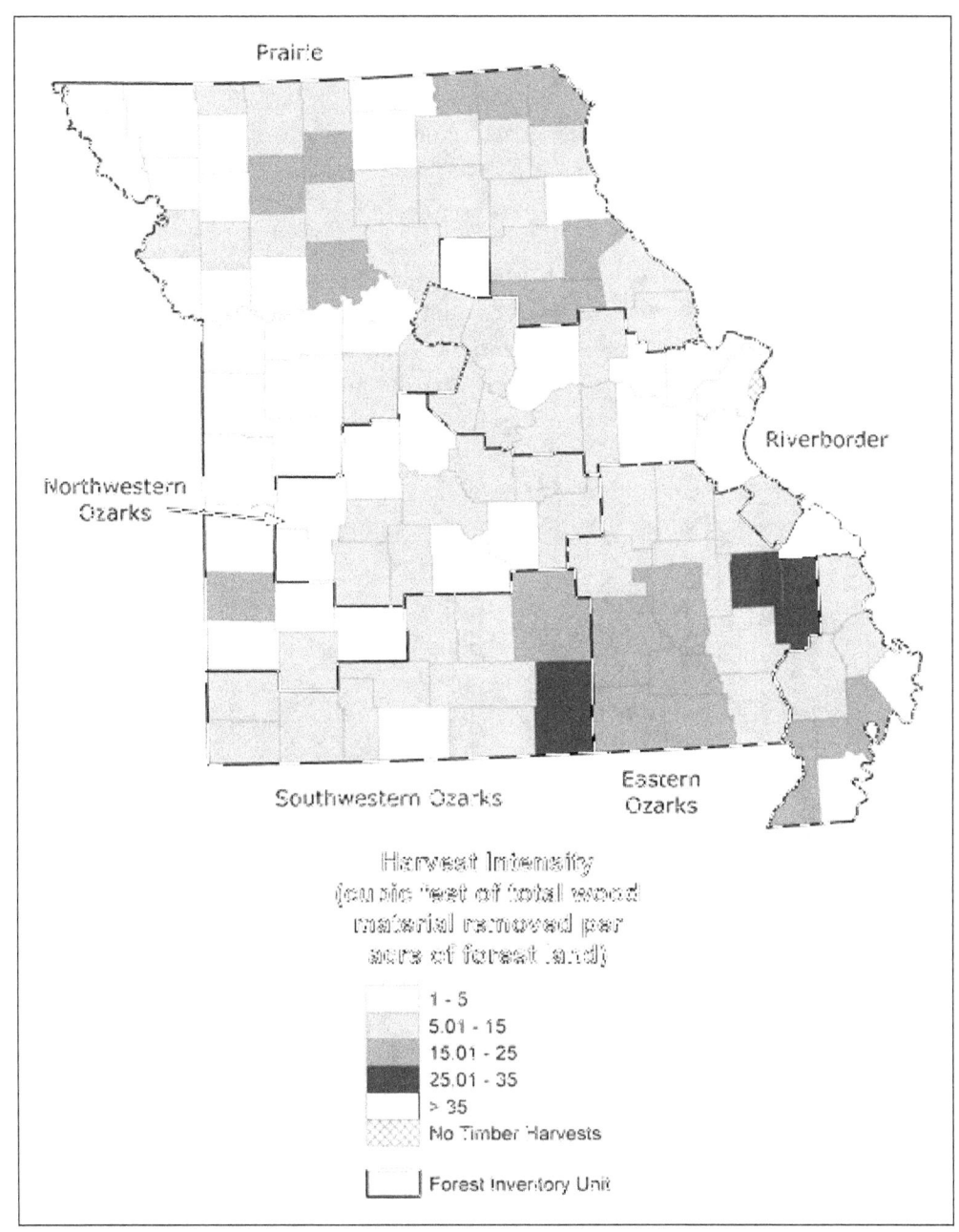

Figure 9.—Harvest intensity for industrial roundwood production, Missouri, 2009.

Primary Mill Residues

- In converting industrial roundwood into products, Missouri's primary wood-using industries generated a combined 1.5 million green tons of coarse wood residue (slabs, edgings, and veneer cores), fine wood residue (sawdust and veneer clippings), and bark residue (Table 14, Fig. 10).

- Thirty-four percent of mill residues generated were used to make charcoal. Fiber products and industrial fuelwood each consumed 11 percent of mill residues; residential fuelwood consumed 5 percent; and all other uses, such as livestock bedding, mulch, and small dimension lumber, consumed 34 percent. Only 5 percent of residues generated went unused (Fig. 11).

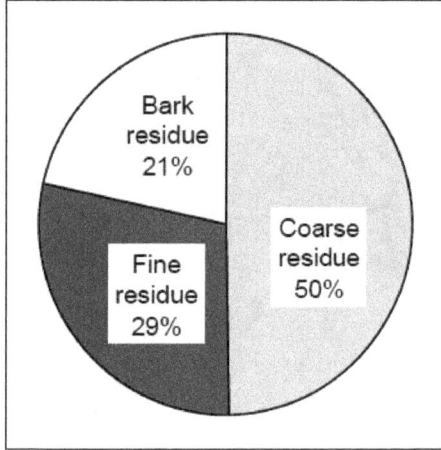

Figure 10.—Distribution of residues generated by primary wood-using mills by type of residue, Missouri, 2009.

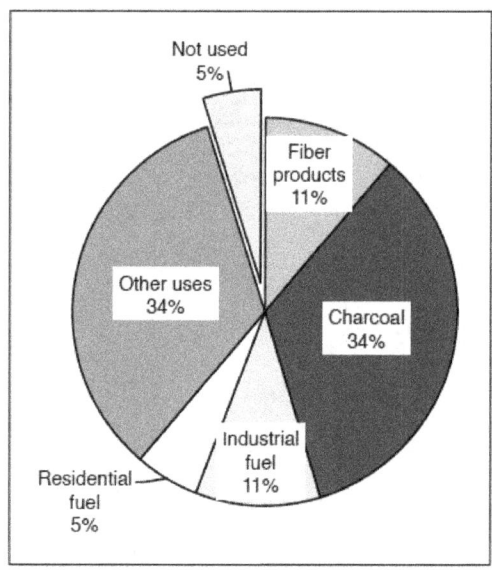

Figure 11.—Distribution of residues generated by primary wood-using mills by method of disposal, Missouri, 2009.

- The most common disposal method for coarse wood residue and sawdust was for the production of charcoal; more than 35 percent of the combined total went for this use. More than 50 percent of the bark residue went for miscellaneous uses such as mulch and animal bedding.

ACKNOWLEDGMENTS

Special thanks are given to the primary wood-using firms for supplying information for this study and to the Missouri Department of Conservation, Forestry Division, whose cooperation in canvassing survey respondents is greatly appreciated.

Figures 2 and 8 were created by Brian Walters, forester with FIA in St. Paul, MN.

LITERATURE CITED

Hackett, R.L.; Jones, S.G.; Piva, R.J. 1993. **Missouri timber industry – assessment of timber product output and use, 1991.** Resour. Bull. NC-151. St. Paul, MN: U.S. Department of Agriculture, Forest Service, North Central Forest Experiment Station. 46 p.

Moser, W.K.; Barnett, C.H.; Hansen, M.H.; Treiman, T.B. 2010. **Missouri's forest resources, 2009.** Res. Note. NRS-80. Newtown Square, PA: U.S. Department of Agriculture, Forest Service, Northern Research Station. 4 p. [Available only online at: http://nrs.fs.fed.us/pubs/36829]

Piva, R.J. In prep. **Pulpwood production in the Northern Region, 2009.** Resour. Bull. Newtown Square, PA: U.S. Department of Agriculture, Forest Service, Northern Research Station. xx p.

Piva, R.J.; Jones, S.G. 1997. **Missouri timber industry – an assessment of timber product output and use, 1994.** Resour. Bull. NC-184. St. Paul, MN: U.S. Department of Agriculture, Forest Service, North Central Forest Experiment Station. 54 p.

Piva, R.J.; Treiman, T.B. 2003. **Missouri timber industry – an assessment of timber product output and use, 2000.** Resour. Bull. NC-223. St. Paul, MN: U.S. Department of Agriculture, Forest Service, North Central Research Station. 75 p.

Piva, R.J.; Jones, S.G.; Barnickol, L.W.; Treiman, T.B. 2000. **Missouri timber industry – an assessment of timber product output and use, 1997.** Resour. Bull. NC-197. St. Paul, MN: U.S. Department of Agriculture, Forest Service, North Central Research Station. 53 p.

Treiman, T.B.; Piva, R.J. 2005. **Missouri timber industry – an assessment of timber product output and use, 2003.** Resour. Bull. NC-250. St. Paul, MN: U.S. Department of Agriculture, Forest Service, North Central Research Station. 74 p.

Treiman, T.B.; Tuttle, J.G.; Piva, R.J. 2008. **Missouri timber industry – an assessment of timber product output and use, 2006.** 75 p. [Available only online at: http://mdc4.mdc.mo.gov/Documents/18636.pdf].

U.S. Census Bureau. 2007. **2007 economic census.** http://www.census.gov/econ/census07/ [Accessed May 2, 2012].

APPENDIX

Definition of Terms

Board foot. Unit of measure applied to roundwood. It relates to lumber that is 1 foot long, 1 foot wide, and 1 inch thick (or its equivalent).

Bolt. A short log no more than 8 feet long, to be sawn for lumber, peeled or sliced for veneer, shaved for excelsior, or converted into shingles, cooperage stock, dimension stock, blocks, blanks, or other products.

Central stem. The portion of a tree between a 1-foot stump and the minimum 4.0-inch top diameter outside bark, or point where the central stem breaks into limbs.

Coarse mill residue. Wood residue suitable for chipping such as slabs, edgings, and veneer cores.

Commercial species. Tree species presently or prospectively suitable for industrial wood products. (Note: Excludes species of typically small size, poor form, or inferior quality such as hophornbeam, Osage-orange, and redbud.)

Cull removals. Net volume of rough and rotten trees plus the net volume in sections of the central stem of growing-stock trees that do not meet regional merchantability standards but are harvested for industrial roundwood products.

Diameter at breast height (d.b.h.). The outside bark diameter at 4.5 feet above the forest floor on the uphill side of the tree. For determining breast height, the forest floor includes the duff layer that may be present, but does not include unincorporated woody debris that may rise above the ground line.

Doyle rule. A simple log rule or formula for estimating the board-foot volume of logs based on a 4-inch slabbing allowance to square the log. This rule is used in the Eastern and Southern United States.

Exports. The volume of roundwood utilized by mills outside the state where the timber was harvested.

Fine mill residue. Wood residue not suitable for chipping, such as sawdust and veneer clippings.

Forest land. Land at least 10-percent stocked with trees of any size, or formerly having had such tree cover, and not currently developed for nonforest use. (Note: Stocking is measured by comparing specified standards with basal area and/or number of trees, age or size, and spacing.) The minimum area for classification of forest land is 1 acre. Roadside, streamside, and shelterbelt strips of timber must have a crown width of at least 120 feet to qualify as forest land. Unimproved roads and trails, streams or other bodies of water, or clearings in forest areas shall be classified as forest if less than 120 feet wide.

Growing-stock removals. The growing-stock volume removed from timberland by harvesting industrial roundwood products. (Note: Includes sawtimber removals, poletimber removals, and logging residues.)

Growing-stock tree. A live timberland tree of commercial species that meets specified standards of size, quality, and merchantability. (Note: Excludes rough, rotten, and dead trees.)

Growing-stock volume. Net volume of growing-stock trees 5.0 inches d.b.h. and larger, from 1 foot above the ground to a minimum 4.0-inch top diameter outside bark of the central stem or to the point where the central stem breaks into limbs.

Hardwoods. Dicotyledonous trees, usually broad-leaved and deciduous.

Harvest residues. The total net volume of unused portions of trees cut or killed by logging. (Note: Includes both logging residues and logging slash.)

Industrial fuelwood. A roundwood product, with or without bark, used to generate energy at manufacturing facilities and schools, correctional institutions, or electric generating plants.

Imports. The volume of roundwood delivered to a mill or group of mills in a specific state but harvested outside that state.

Industrial roundwood exports. The quantity of industrial roundwood harvested in a geographical area and transported to other geographical areas.

Industrial roundwood imports. The quantity of industrial roundwood received from other geographical areas.

Industrial roundwood products. Saw logs, pulpwood, veneer logs, poles, commercial posts, pilings, cooperage logs, particleboard bolts, shaving bolts, lath bolts, charcoal bolts, and chips from roundwood used for pulp or board products.

Industrial roundwood production. The quantity of industrial roundwood harvested in a geographic area plus all industrial roundwood exported to other geographical areas.

Industrial roundwood receipts. The quantity of industrial roundwood received by commercial mills in a geographic area plus all industrial roundwood imported from other geographical areas.

Industrial roundwood retained. The quantity of industrial roundwood harvested from and processed by commercial mills within the same geographical area.

International ¼-inch rule. A log rule or formula for estimating the board-foot volume of logs, allowing ½ inch of taper for each 4-foot length and assuming ¼ inch of kerf. This rule is used as the U.S. Forest Service standard log rule in the Eastern United States.

Limbwood removals. Net volume of all portions of a tree other than the central stem (including forks, large limbs, tops, and stumps) harvested for industrial roundwood products.

Logging residue. The net volume of unused portions of the merchantable central stem of growing-stock trees cut or killed by logging.

Logging slash. The net volume of unused portions of the unmerchantable (non-growing-stock) sections of trees cut or killed by logging.

Merchantable sections. Refers to sections of the central stem of growing-stock trees that meet either pulpwood or saw log specifications.

Net volume. Gross volume less deductions for rot, sweep, or other defects affecting use for roundwood products.

Noncommercial species. Trees species of typically small size, poor form, or inferior quality that normally do not develop into trees suitable for industrial roundwood products. Noncommercial species are listed in the volume tables as rough trees.

Nonforest land. Land that has never supported forests, and land formerly forested where use for timber management is precluded by development for other uses. (Note: Includes areas used for crops, active Christmas tree plantations, orchards, nurseries, improved pasture, residential areas, city parks, improved roads of any width and adjoining clearings, powerline clearings of any width, and 1- to 39.9-acre areas of water classified by the Bureau of the Census as land.) If intermingled in forest areas, unimproved roads and nonforest strips must be more than 120 feet wide and more than 1 acre to qualify as nonforest land.

Nonforest land removals. Net volume of trees on nonforest lands harvested for industrial roundwood products.

Poletimber. A growing-stock tree at least 5.0 inches d.b.h. but smaller than sawtimber size (9.0 inches d.b.h. for softwoods, 11.0 inches d.b.h. for hardwoods).

Poletimber removals. Net volume in the merchantable central stem of poletimber trees harvested for industrial roundwood products.

Primary wood-using mills. Mills receiving roundwood or chips from roundwood for processing into products such as lumber, veneer, and pulp.

Primary wood-using mill residue. Wood materials (coarse and fine) and bark generated at manufacturing plants that process industrial roundwood into principal products. These residues include wood products obtained incidental to production of principal products and wood materials not utilized for some product.

Production. The quantity of roundwood material harvested in a geographic area plus all roundwood material exported to other geographical areas.

Receipts. The quantity of roundwood material received by commercial mills in a geographic area plus all roundwood material imported from other geographical areas.

Retained. Roundwood volume harvested from and processed by mills within the same state.

Rotten tree. A tree that does not meet regional merchantability standards because of excessive unsound cull.

Rough tree. A tree that does not meet regional merchantability standards because of excessive sound cull (includes forks, sweep and crook, and large branches or knots), including noncommercial tree species.

Roundwood. Logs, bolts, or other round sections cut from trees (including chips from roundwood).

Sapling. A live tree between 1.0 and 5.0 inches d.b.h.

Saw log portion. That portion of the central stem of sawtimber trees between the stump and the saw log top.

Saw log top. The point on the central stem of sawtimber trees above which a saw log cannot be produced. The minimum saw log top is 7.0 inches diameter outside bark for softwoods and 9.0 inches diameter outside bark for hardwoods.

Sawtimber removals. As used in Table 10, sawtimber removals refers to the net volume in the merchantable central stem of sawtimber-size trees harvested for industrial roundwood products. (Note: includes the saw log and upper stem portions of sawtimber-size trees.) When referring to the sawtimber volume removed from timberland as in Table 12, sawtimber removals refers to the net volume in the saw log portion of sawtimber-size trees harvested for roundwood products or left on the ground as harvest residue, and is usually expressed in thousands of board feet (International ¼-inch rule).

Sawtimber tree. A growing-stock tree containing at least a 12-foot saw log or two noncontiguous saw logs 8 feet or longer, and meeting regional specifications for freedom from defect. Softwoods must be at least 9.0 inches d.b.h. and hardwoods must be at least 11.0 inches d.b.h.

Sawtimber volume. Net volume in the saw log portion of sawtimber trees.

Softwoods. Coniferous trees, usually evergreen, having needles or scale-like leaves.

Timber product output. The volume of roundwood products produced from an area's forests.

Timberland. Forest land that is producing, or is capable of producing, in excess of 20 cubic feet per acre per year of industrial roundwood products under natural conditions, is not withdrawn from timber utilization by statute or administrative regulation, and is not associated with urban or rural development.

Tree. A woody perennial plant, typically large, with a single well-defined stem carrying a more or less definite crown; sometimes defined as attaining a minimum diameter of 3 in. (7.6 cm) and a minimum height of 15 ft (4.6 m) at maturity. For FIA, any plant on the tree list in the current field manual is measured as a tree.

Upper stem portion. That portion of the central stem of sawtimber trees between the saw log top and the minimum top diameter of 4.0 inches outside bark, or to the point where the central stem breaks into limbs.

Common and Scientific Names of Tree Species by Species Group

Softwoods

Eastern redcedar	*Juniperus virginiana*
Shortleaf pine	*Pinus echinata*
White pine	*Pinus strobus*
Other Pines	
Austrian pine	*Pinus nigra*
Scotch pine	*Pinus sylvestris*
Virginia pine	*Pinus virginiana*
Bald cypress	*Taxodium distichum*

Hardwoods

Ash	
White ash	*Fraxinus americana*
Black ash	*Fraxinus nigra*

Green ash	*Fraxinus pennsylvanica*
Blue ash	*Fraxinus quadrangulata*
American basswood	*Tilia americana*
American beech	*Fagus grandifolia*
River birch	*Betula nigra*
Black cherry	*Prunus serotina*
Black walnut	*Juglans nigra*
Eastern cottonwood	*Populus deltoides*

Elm

Winged elm	*Ulmus alata*
American elm	*Ulmus americana*
Siberian elm	*Ulmus pumila*
Slippery elm	*Ulmus rubra*
Rock elm	*Ulmus thomasii*

Hickory

Mockernut hickory	*Carya alba*
Bitternut hickory	*Carya cordiformis*
Pignut hickory	*Carya glabra*
Pecan	*Carya illinoensis*
Shellbark hickory	*Carya laciniosa*
Shagbark hickory	*Carya ovata*
Black hickory	*Carya texana*

Hard maple

    Black maple   *Acer nigrum*

    Sugar maple   *Acer saccharum*

Soft maple

    Boxelder   *Acer negundo*

    Red maple   *Acer rubrum*

    Silver maple   *Acer saccharinum*

Red oak group

    Scarlet oak   *Quercus coccinea*

    Northern pin oak   *Quercus ellipsoidalis*

    Southern red oak   *Quercus falcata*

    Cherrybark oak   *Quercus falcata var. pagodifolia*

    Shingle oak   *Quercus imbricaria*

    Blackjack oak   *Quercus marilandica*

    Pin oak   *Quercus palustris*

    Willow oak   *Quercus phellos*

    Northern red oak   *Quercus rubra*

    Shumard oak   *Quercus shumardii var. shumardii*

    Black oak   *Quercus velutina*

White oak group

    White oak   *Quercus alba*

    Swamp white oak   *Quercus bicolor*

    Overcup oak   *Quercus lyrata*

Bur oak	*Quercus macrocarpa*
Swamp chestnut oak	*Quercus michauxii*
Chinkapin oak	*Quercus muehlenbergii*
Chestnut oak	*Quercus prinus*
Post oak	*Quercus stellata*
Sweetgum	*Liquidambar styraciflua*
American sycamore	*Platanus occidentalis*
Tupelo/gum	
Water tupelo	*Quercus aquatica*
Swamp tupelo	*Nyssa sylvatica var. biflora*
Blackgum (black tupelo)	*Nyssa sylvatica var. sylvatica*
Yellow-poplar	*Liriodendron tulipifera*
Other hardwoods	
Ohio buckeye	*Aesculus glabra*
Ailanthus	*Ailanthus altissima*
Mimosa, silktree	*Albizia julibrissin*
Serviceberry	*Amelanchier sp.*
Pawpaw	*Asimina triloba*
Chittamwood, gum bumelia	*Bumelia lanuginosa*
American hornbeam, musclewood	*Carpinus caroliniana*
Northern catalpa	*Catalpa speciosa*
Sugarberry	*Celtis laevigata*
Hackberry	*Celtis occidentalis*

Eastern redbud	*Cercis canadensis*
Flowering dogwood	*Cornus florida*
Hawthorn spp.	*Crataegus spp.*
Common persimmon	*Diospyros virginiana*
Waterlocust	*Gleditsia aquatica*
Honeylocust	*Gleditsia triacanthos*
Kentucky coffeetree	*Gymnocladus dioicus*
Butternut	*Juglans cinerea*
Osage-orange	*Maclura pomifera*
Apple spp.	*Malus spp.*
White mulberry	*Morus alba*
Red mulberry	*Morus rubra*
Eastern hophornbeam	*Ostrya virginiana*
American plum, wild plum	*Prunus americana*
Black locust	*Robinia pseudoacacia*
Peachleaf willow	*Salix amygdaloides*
Black willow	*Salix nigra*
Sassafras	*Sassafras albidum*

Tables

Table 1.–Conversion factors from reported unit of measure to standard unit of measure (This table is in the Study Methods section.)

Table 2.–Number of active primary wood-using mills by mill type and survey year, Missouri

Table 3.–Industrial roundwood receipts, in million cubic feet, by mill type, softwoods and hardwoods, and survey year, Missouri

Table 4.–Industrial roundwood receipts, in thousand cubic feet, by species group and state of origin, Missouri, 2009

Table 5.–Industrial roundwood production, in million cubic feet, by product, softwoods and hardwoods, and survey year, Missouri

Table 6.–Industrial roundwood production, in thousand cubic feet, by species group and state of destination, Missouri, 2009

Table 7.–Industrial roundwood production, in thousand cubic feet, by Forest Inventory Unit, county, and species group, Missouri, 2009

Table 8.–Industrial roundwood production by Forest Inventory Unit, species group, and product, Missouri, 2009

Table 9.–Saw log receipts and production, in thousand board feet, by Forest Inventory Unit and species group, Missouri, 2006 and 2009

Table 10.–Wood material harvested for industrial roundwood, in thousand cubic feet, by Forest Inventory Unit, source of material, and species group, Missouri, 2009

Table 11.–Growing-stock removals from timberland for industrial roundwood, in thousand cubic feet, by Forest Inventory Unit, county, and species group, Missouri, 2009

Table 12.–Sawtimber removals from timberland for industrial roundwood, in thousand board feet, by Forest Inventory Unit, county, and species group, Missouri, 2009

Table 13.–Harvest residue generated by industrial roundwood harvesting, in thousand cubic feet, by Forest Inventory Unit, county, and species group, Missouri, 2009

Table 14.–Disposition of residues produced at primary wood-using mills, in thousand green tons, by Forest Inventory Unit, disposition, residue type, and softwoods and hardwoods, Missouri, 2009

Table 2.—Number of active primary wood-using mills by mill type and survey year, Missouri

Mill type and mill size	Survey Year											
	1946	1958	1969	1980	1987	1991	1994	1997	2000	2003	2006	2009
Sawmills												
Large[a]	2	5	7	8	13	17	32	35	31	34	38	25
Medium[b]	43	103	117	163	169	172	189	212	185	170	151	144
Small[c]	2,548	882	425	315	228	206	191	170	187	167	167	197
Total	2,593	990	549	486	410	395	412	417	403	371	356	366
Other Mills												
Cooperage mills	85	36	36	30	20	20	12	8	9	8	8	9
Veneer mills	6	3	4	4	5	4	1	1	1	1	--	--
Pulp mills	--	2	2	2	1	1	1	1	1	1	1	1
Charcoal[d]	3	60	52	36	15	14	14	10	6	4	4	5
Handle mills	19	12	7	10	6	6	5	6	4	5	4	1
Post and pole mills	6	14	22	28	23	17	9	7	7	8	8	9
Other products[e]	94	44	9	3	11	14	7	5	9	6	8	10
Total	213	171	132	113	81	76	49	38	37	33	33	35
All mills	2,806	1,161	681	599	491	471	461	455	440	404	389	401

[a] Annual lumber production in excess of 5 million board feet.
[b] Annual lumber production from 1 million to 5 million board feet.
[c] Annual lumber production less than 1 million board feet.
[d] Includes only those charcoal operations using roundwood.
[e] Includes plants producing excelsior, cabin logs, mine timbers, etc.

Table 3.—Industrial roundwood receipts, in million cubic feet, by mill type, and softwoods and hardwoods, and survey year, Missouri

Product	Survey Year							2006 - 2009
	1991	1994	1997	2000	2003	2006	2009	% change
ALL SPECIES								
Sawmills	100.1	124.2	128.5	118.4	117.2	114.3	95.0	-1
Charcoal	4.6	2.4	1.2	0.9	0.6	0.7	0.1	-8
Cooperage mills	5.0	4.6	6.1	4.0	5.3	8.5	5.2	-3
Post and pole mills	3.0	1.1	1.5	0.9	1.1	1.3	0.9	-3
Other mills[a]	3.4	3.3	3.2	3.0	2.0	4.9	1.7	-6
Total	116.2	135.5	140.5	127.2	126.2	129.7	102.9	-2
SOFTWOODS								
Sawmills	7.7	9.7	9.5	6.5	5.0	5.7	5.0	-1
Charcoal	0.0	0.0	0.0	--	--	--	--	--
Cooperage mills	--	--	--	--	--	--	--	--
Post and pole mills	2.6	0.9	1.1	0.8	1.1	1.3	0.8	-3
Other mills[a]	1.2	1.9	1.2	1.6	1.0	1.7	1.0	-4
Total	11.5	12.4	11.9	8.9	7.1	8.7	6.9	-2
HARDWOODS								
Sawmills	92.4	114.5	119.0	111.9	112.1	108.6	90.0	-1
Charcoal	4.6	2.4	1.2	0.9	0.6	0.7	0.1	-8
Cooperage mills	5.0	4.6	6.1	4.0	5.3	8.5	5.2	-3
Post and pole mills	0.5	0.2	0.3	0.1	0.0	0.1	0.0	-3
Other mills[a]	2.2	1.5	2.0	1.4	1.0	3.2	0.6	-7
Total	104.7	123.1	128.6	118.2	119.1	121.1	96.0	-2

All table cells without observations are indicated by -- . Table value of 0.0 indicates the volume rounds to less than 0.1 thousand cubic feet. Columns and rows may not add to their totals due to rounding.

a Includes mills producing excelsior, pulpwood, veneer, cabin logs, etc.

Table 4.—Industrial roundwood receipts, in thousand cubic feet, by species group and state of origin, Missouri, 2009

Species group	Total	Arkansas	Illinois	Indiana	Iowa	Kansas	Kentucky	Missouri	Nebraska	Oklahoma	Tennessee	Other States[a]
Softwoods												
Eastern redcedar	3,394	149	31	--	--	0	--	3,214	--	--	--	--
Cypress	10	--	--	--	--	--	--	10	--	--	--	--
Shortleaf pine	3,502	99	1	--	--	--	--	3,402	--	--	--	--
White pine	4	--	3	--	--	--	--	2	--	--	--	--
Total	6,910	248	35	--	--	0	--	6,628	--	--	--	--
Hardwoods												
Ash	1,187	5	42	11	3	2	6	1,116	--	--	4	--
Basswood	0	--	--	--	--	--	--	0	--	--	--	--
River birch	46	--	--	--	--	--	--	46	--	--	--	--
Black cherry	138	4	19	8	0	0	5	100	--	--	3	--
Black walnut	5,011	456	56	5	42	462	3	3,853	4	127	2	--
Cottonwood	2,668	1	156	--	20	12	--	2,475	4	--	--	--
Elm	276	2	0	--	1	0	--	272	--	--	--	--
Hickory	4,799	109	84	32	6	5	42	4,505	--	2	13	--
Hard maple	423	4	44	11	0	--	6	354	--	--	4	--
Soft maple	1,576	1	272	--	217	5	5	1,080	1	--	--	--
Red oak group	49,594	1,014	679	107	40	21	66	47,568	1	56	41	--
White oak group	27,580	574	771	417	61	16	91	25,188	0	16	135	310
Sweet gum	98	2	0	--	--	--	--	96	--	--	--	--
Sycamore	1,508	5	31	--	2	2	--	1,465	0	2	--	--
Tupelo/gum	112	2	--	--	--	--	--	111	--	--	--	--
Yellow-poplar	604	12	150	35	--	--	21	374	--	--	12	--
Other hardwoods	346	1	0	--	0	1	--	344	--	--	--	--
Total	95,966	2,192	2,304	625	392	527	241	88,947	11	204	214	310
State total	102,876	2,439	2,339	625	392	527	241	95,575	11	204	214	310

All table cells without observations are indicated by -- . Table value of 0 indicates the volume rounds to less than 1 thousand cubic feet. Columns and rows may not add to their totals due to rounding.

[a] Includes Ohio, West Virginia, and Wisconsin.

Table 5.—Industrial roundwood production, in million cubic feet, by product, softwoods and hardwoods, and survey year, Missouri

Product	Survey Year													2006 - 2009
	1946	1958	1969	1980	1987	1991	1994	1997	2000	2003	2006	2009	% change
	ALL SPECIES												
Saw logs	79.4	47.8	66.3	71.7	89.7	93.7	120.0	125.0	113.1	111.2	110.1	92.3	-16%
Veneer logs	1.4	1.0	1.0	0.7	1.0	1.7	1.1	0.9	0.7	1.3	1.0	0.9	-10%
Pulpwood	0.6	0.8	1.9	1.9	2.2	1.2	1.5	4.3	8.5	7.2	3.0	3.0	2%
Charcoal	0.6	3.2	16.7	6.2	2.7	4.6	2.4	1.2	0.8	0.6	0.7	0.1	-83%
Cooperage logs	14.9	4.5	8.9	4.7	2.0	4.8	4.2	5.1	3.3	4.9	5.3	3.8	-28%
Handle bolts	1.3	1.2	0.4	--	0.1	0.2	0.2	0.3	0.1	0.2	0.1	0.1	7%
Poles	0.0	0.2	0.3	--	0.1	--	--	--	0.1	--	0.6	0.6	0%
Posts	11.0	9.6	2.5	1.7	1.3	3.1	1.1	1.4	0.8	1.1	0.7	0.2	-68%
Industrial fuelwood	59.4	61.9	24.5	--	--	0.0	--	--	--	--	--	0.2	--
Other products[a]	5.6	6.2	1.1	0.6	0.8	12.1	2.1	1.3	1.7	1.0	4.1	1.3	-68%
Total	174.2	136.4	123.6	87.5	99.9	121.4	132.6	139.6	129.0	127.6	125.5	102.6	-18%
	SOFTWOODS												
Saw logs	8.3	4.1	3.3	5.5	7.8	7.5	9.3	9.5	6.5	4.7	5.7	5.4	-6%
Veneer logs	--	--	--	--	--	--	0.0	0.0	--	0.0	--	--	--
Pulpwood	0.1	0.1	--	--	--	--	0.0	0.1	--	0.2	0.0	0.3	>500%[b]
Charcoal	--	--	--	--	--	--	0.0	0.0	--	--	--	--	--
Cooperage logs	--	--	--	--	--	--	--	--	--	--	--	--	--
Handle bolts	--	--	--	--	0.0	--	--	--	--	--	--	--	--
Poles	0.0	0.2	0.3	--	0.0	--	--	--	0.1	--	0.5	0.5	2%
Posts	3.2	0.8	1.2	0.5	0.7	2.6	0.9	1.1	0.7	1.1	0.7	0.2	-68%
Industrial fuelwood	0.2	0.2	0.1	--	--	0.0	--	--	--	--	--	0.0	--
Other products[a]	0.0	0.0	0.3	0.2	0.6	1.7	1.8	1.1	1.5	0.9	1.7	1.0	-39%
Total	11.8	5.4	5.2	6.2	9.1	11.8	12.1	11.9	8.8	6.9	8.7	7.5	-14%

(Table 5 continued on next page)

27

Table 5.—Continued

HARDWOODS

Saw logs	71.1	43.7	63.0	66.2	81.9	86.2	110.7	115.5	106.6	106.5	104.3	86.9	-17%
Veneer logs	1.4	1.0	1.0	0.7	1.0	1.7	1.1	0.9	0.7	1.3	1.0	0.9	-10%
Pulpwood	0.5	0.7	1.9	1.9	2.2	1.2	1.5	4.2	8.5	7.0	3.0	2.7	-8%
Charcoal	0.6	3.2	16.7	6.2	2.7	4.6	2.4	1.2	0.8	0.6	0.7	0.1	-83%
Cooperage logs	14.9	4.5	8.9	4.7	2.0	4.8	4.2	5.1	3.3	4.9	5.3	3.8	-28%
Handle bolts	1.3	1.2	0.4	--	0.1	0.2	0.2	0.3	0.1	0.2	0.1	0.1	7%
Poles	--	--	0.0	--	0.1	--	--	--	--	--	0.0	0.0	-30%
Posts	7.8	8.8	1.3	1.2	0.6	0.5	0.2	0.3	0.1	0.0	0.0	0.0	-86%
Industrial fuelwood	59.2	61.7	24.4	--	--	--	--	--	--	--	--	--	-88%
Other products[a]	5.6	6.2	0.8	0.4	0.2	10.4	0.3	0.2	0.2	0.1	2.4	0.3	-88%
Total	162.4	131.0	118.4	81.3	90.8	109.6	120.5	127.7	120.2	120.7	116.8	95.1	-19%

All table cells without observations are indicated by --. Table value of 0.0 indicates the volume rounds to less than 0.1 thousand cubic feet. Columns and rows may not add to their totals due to rounding.

[a] Includes excelsior, cabin logs, and other miscellaneous products.

[b] Volumes are too small to calculate a meaningful percent change.

Table 6.—Industrial roundwood production, in thousand cubic feet, by species group and state of mill, Missouri, 2009

Species group	Total	State of mill									Okla-homa	Other foreign
		Arkansas	Illinois	Indiana	Iowa	Kansas	Kentucky	Michigan	Missouri	Nebraska		
Softwoods												
Eastern redcedar	3,214	--	--	--	--	--	--	--	3,214	--	--	--
Cypress	10	--	--	--	--	--	--	--	10	--	--	--
Shortleaf pine	4,272	567	--	--	--	--	302	--	3,402	--	--	--
White pine	2	--	--	--	--	--	--	--	2	--	--	--
Other pine	2	--	--	--	--	--	2	--	--	--	--	--
Total	7,499	567	--	--	--	--	304	--	6,628	--	--	--
Hardwoods												
Ash	1,284	--	118	--	14	11	20	--	1,116	--	6	--
Basswood	14	--	--	--	13	--	--	--	0	--	--	--
River birch	46	--	--	--	--	--	0	--	46	--	--	--
Black cherry	134	--	--	3	10	--	17	--	100	--	1	--
Black walnut	5,224	--	70	8	950	1	--	--	3,853	8	8	326
Cottonwood	2,529	--	0	--	43	2	9	--	2,475	--	--	--
Elm	354	--	2	--	5	--	71	--	272	--	4	--
Hickory	4,749	0	14	--	10	1	212	--	4,505	1	--	6
Hard maple	388	--	1	7	1	--	25	--	354	--	--	--
Soft maple	1,374	--	2	--	264	17	4	--	1,080	--	--	7
Red oak group	48,950	1	112	4	257	6	940	--	47,568	--	27	35
White oak group	27,210	1	20	13	266	18	937	431	25,188	2	80	254
Sweet gum	149	--	--	--	--	--	52	--	96	--	--	--
Sycamore	1,485	--	2	--	--	1	14	--	1,465	--	3	--
Tupelo/gum	130	--	--	--	--	--	19	--	111	--	--	--
Yellow-poplar	397	--	--	--	--	--	23	--	374	--	--	--
Other hardwoods	710	--	0	--	--	2	359	--	344	--	4	--
Total	95,125	2	344	36	1,832	59	2,702	431	88,947	11	134	628
Grand Total	102,624	569	344	36	1,832	59	3,006	431	95,575	11	134	628

All table cells without observations are indicated by --. Table value of 0 indicates the volume rounds to less than 1 thousand cubic feet. Columns and rows may not add to their totals due to rounding.

Table 7.—Industrial roundwood production, in thousand cubic feet, by Forest Inventory Unit, county, and species group, Missouri, 2009

Forest Inventory Unit and county	All species	Softwoods						Hardwoods				
		Eastern redcedar	Cypress	Shortleaf pine	White pine	Other pine	Total softwoods	Ash	Basswood	River birch	Black cherry	Black walnut
Eastern Ozark Unit												
Bollinger	2,652	2	--	33	--	--	35	184	--	--	20	30
Butler	1,005	--	1	92	--	--	93	1	--	--	--	3
Carter	3,827	--	--	324	--	--	324	7	--	--	0	4
Crawford	2,054	6	--	52	--	--	58	5	--	0	0	25
Dent	2,132	20	--	79	--	--	98	2	--	--	--	43
Iron	2,515	47	--	55	--	--	103	2	--	--	0	2
Madison	4,868	33	--	261	--	--	293	32	--	--	8	12
Oregon	4,259	22	--	241	--	--	263	34	--	--	1	26
Reynolds	4,674	31	--	193	--	--	224	2	--	--	--	21
Ripley	3,584	81	--	331	--	--	412	10	--	0	1	3
Shannon	6,807	45	--	744	--	--	789	6	--	--	0	83
St. Francois	847	73	--	53	--	--	126	12	--	--	8	9
Washington	3,532	40	--	183	--	--	223	2	--	--	2	4
Wayne	2,306	9	1	167	--	--	177	13	--	--	1	6
Total	45,062	409	1	2,809	--	--	3,219	311	--	0	41	270
Southwestern Ozark Unit												
Barry	1,374	44	--	91	--	--	134	22	--	--	0	137
Christian	870	46	--	19	--	--	66	14	--	--	--	34
Douglas	2,393	62	--	117	--	--	179	1	--	--	--	73
Howell	5,229	21	--	408	--	--	430	9	--	--	7	61
McDonald	1,348	1	--	41	--	--	42	16	--	--	0	103
Newton	792	1	--	4	--	--	5	7	--	--	1	225
Ozark	1,113	177	--	141	--	--	318	0	--	--	1	5
Stone	708	12	--	9	--	--	21	21	--	--	0	148
Taney	887	408	--	30	--	--	438	--	--	--	0	20
Texas	5,061	7	--	458	--	--	465	4	--	--	0	164
Webster	440	34	--	--	--	--	34	0	--	--	--	77
Wright	876	7	--	9	--	--	16	1	--	--	--	89
Total	21,090	820	--	1,326	--	--	2,146	98	--	--	10	1,135

Table 7.—Continued

Forest Inventory Unit and county	All species	Softwoods						Hardwoods				
		Eastern redcedar	Cypress	Shortleaf pine	White pine	Other pine	Total soft-woods	Ash	Bass-wood	River birch	Black cherry	Black walnut
Northwestern Ozark Unit												
Benton	192	11	--	--	--	--	11	2	--	0	--	61
Camden	870	207	--	--	--	--	207	7	--	--	0	42
Cedar	108	--	--	--	--	--	--	15	--	--	0	38
Dallas	737	149	--	--	--	--	149	17	--	--	0	47
Hickory	742	25	--	--	--	--	25	2	--	--	0	86
Laclede	334	84	--	2	--	--	86	0	--	--	0	38
Maries	830	142	--	--	--	--	142	13	--	--	0	24
Miller	1,394	290	--	--	--	--	290	11	--	--	0	58
Morgan	419	37	--	--	--	--	37	3	--	1	0	44
Phelps	1,948	70	--	24	--	--	94	7	--	--	--	59
Polk	510	24	--	--	--	--	24	92	--	--	--	102
Pulaski	388	70	--	4	--	--	74	1	--	--	--	64
St. Clair	231	0	--	--	--	--	0	4	--	0	0	92
Total	8,702	1,109	--	31	--	--	1,139	175	--	1	1	754
Prairie Unit												
Adair	421	--	--	--	--	--	--	2	6	--	1	166
Andrew	56	--	--	--	--	--	--	0	--	--	--	4
Atchison	20	--	--	--	--	--	--	--	--	--	--	14
Audrain	623	0	--	--	--	--	0	23	--	--	0	44
Barton	745	--	--	--	--	--	--	75	--	--	0	11
Bates	128	0	--	--	--	--	0	8	--	0	1	35
Buchanan	228	--	--	--	--	--	--	--	--	--	--	106
Caldwell	103	--	--	--	--	--	--	3	--	--	--	9
Carroll	354	--	--	--	--	--	--	12	--	--	--	0
Cass	283	0	--	--	--	--	0	3	--	--	0	3
Chariton	472	--	--	--	--	--	--	7	--	0	--	40
Clark	945	--	--	--	--	--	--	30	--	12	1	86
Clay	13	--	--	--	--	--	--	1	1	--	2	--
Clinton	27	--	--	--	--	--	--	0	--	--	--	13
Cooper	276	39	--	1	--	--	40	2	--	1	0	62

(Table 7 continued on next page)

31

Table 7.—Continued

Prairie Unit (cont.)

Dade	130	--	--	--	--	15	--	--	--	56
Daviess	540	--	--	--	--	26	--	--	0	45
De Kalb	56	--	--	--	--	1	--	--	--	13
Gentry	123	--	--	--	--	1	--	--	--	14
Greene	305	3	--	3	--	22	--	--	0	111
Grundy	380	--	--	--	--	19	--	--	--	45
Harrison	312	--	--	--	--	14	--	--	--	61
Henry	193	2	--	2	0	9	--	--	0	17
Holt	35	--	--	--	--	--	--	0	--	7
Jasper	163	--	--	--	--	11	--	--	0	43
Johnson	122	2	--	2	--	5	--	--	--	6
Knox	306	--	--	--	--	5	4	--	1	36
Lafayette	62	--	--	--	--	2	--	--	0	0
Lawrence	766	--	--	0	--	33	--	--	0	181
Lewis	581	0	--	1	--	16	--	--	1	87
Lincoln	592	0	1	1	--	19	2	--	1	17
Linn	123	--	--	--	--	2	--	--	0	26
Livingston	245	--	--	--	--	8	--	--	0	33
Macon	410	1	--	1	--	6	0	1	0	6
Marion	134	--	--	--	--	2	--	--	0	18
Mercer	210	--	--	--	--	12	--	--	0	36
Monroe	429	--	--	--	--	4	--	3	0	29
Nodaway	79	--	--	--	--	0	--	--	--	8
Pettis	407	38	--	38	--	5	--	1	0	140
Pike	651	0	--	0	--	36	--	--	0	16
Putnam	103	--	--	--	--	0	--	--	0	29
Ralls	547	--	--	--	--	22	--	--	0	17
Randolph	1,479	--	--	--	--	21	--	17	2	44
Ray	81	--	--	--	--	4	--	--	--	0
Saline	172	--	--	--	--	4	--	--	0	60
Schuyler	501	--	--	--	--	0	--	--	3	344
Scotland	563	--	--	--	--	5	--	--	4	150
Shelby	249	0	--	0	--	6	--	--	0	4
Sullivan	108	--	--	--	--	6	--	--	0	29
Vernon	242	0	--	0	--	6	--	0	0	136
Worth	40	--	--	--	--	0	--	--	0	7
Total	**16,134**	**87**	**1**	**1**	**88**	**508**	**14**	**35**	**18**	**2,462**

Table 7.—Continued

Forest Inventory Unit and county	All species	Softwoods						Hardwoods				
		Eastern redcedar	Cypress	Shortleaf pine	White pine	Other pine	Total soft- woods	Ash	Bass- wood	River birch	Black cherry	Black walnut
Riverborder Unit												
Boone	560	0	--	--	--	--	0	7	--	7	1	82
Callaway	374	31	--	--	--	--	31	0	--	--	0	53
Cape Girardeau	814	10	--	11	--	--	21	21	--	--	9	23
Cole	511	95	--	1	--	--	96	10	--	--	0	18
Dunklin	73	--	0	2	--	--	2	5	--	--	--	1
Franklin	735	14	--	6	--	--	20	10	--	--	0	33
Gasconade	984	120	--	1	--	--	122	10	--	--	0	9
Howard	267	--	--	--	--	--	--	5	--	2	0	56
Jefferson	511	66	--	19	--	2	88	11	--	--	8	4
Mississippi	2	--	--	--	--	--	--	--	--	--	--	--
Moniteau	421	80	--	3	--	--	83	4	--	--	0	66
Montgomery	554	101	--	--	--	--	101	17	--	--	0	13
New Madrid	460	--	1	--	--	--	1	2	--	--	--	1
Osage	1,144	163	--	--	--	--	163	22	--	--	0	8
Pemiscot	1	--	--	--	--	--	--	--	--	--	--	--
Perry	2,502	23	--	20	--	--	42	53	--	--	33	169
Scott	76	--	0	--	--	--	0	0	--	--	0	1
St. Charles	138	1	--	1	0	--	2	1	--	--	2	11
St. Louis	31	1	--	--	--	--	1	0	--	--	0	4
Ste. Genevieve	686	70	--	39	--	--	108	13	--	--	8	22
Stoddard	428	--	8	3	--	--	11	0	--	--	1	11
Warren	364	14	--	0	1	--	15	3	--	--	2	19
Total	11,636	789	9	105	1	2	906	193	14	9	64	602
State total	102,624	3,214	10	4,272	2	2	7,499	1,284	14	46	134	5,224

(Table 7 continued on next page)

Table 7.—Continued

Forest Inventory Unit and county	Cotton-wood	Elm	Hickory	Hard maple	Soft maple	Red oak group	White oak group	Sweet-gum	Syca-more	Tupelo/gum	Yellow-poplar	Other hard-woods	Total hard-woods
Eastern Ozark Unit													
Bollinger	10	4	272	85	7	1,172	772	9	14	3	37	0	2,617
Butler	1	5	68	--	9	571	229	9	10	7	--	--	913
Carter	0	10	207	--	27	2,307	912	3	14	13	--	0	3,502
Crawford	6	7	76	7	6	1,122	713	1	25	1	--	2	1,996
Dent	5	1	122	1	5	1,158	676	0	18	--	--	1	2,033
Iron	3	0	91	4	7	1,554	735	0	10	4	--	0	2,412
Madison	7	7	351	57	7	2,387	1,603	14	41	25	24	0	4,574
Oregon	12	39	274	5	2	2,451	1,122	0	27	3	--	--	3,996
Reynolds	--	2	249	0	3	3,027	1,110	--	32	4	--	--	4,450
Ripley	5	14	188	1	14	2,066	815	19	25	7	--	4	3,172
Shannon	0	3	359	0	6	4,146	1,399	--	11	4	--	0	6,018
St. Francois	8	--	39	13	--	383	224	0	3	1	21	0	721
Washington	13	9	93	14	5	2,219	907	1	31	2	--	6	3,310
Wayne	0	5	183	14	7	1,193	673	6	18	10	--	0	2,129
Total	72	107	2,571	201	106	25,755	11,892	62	278	83	81	14	41,843
Southwestern Ozark Unit													
Barry	--	0	79	--	0	670	304	--	24	2	--	1	1,240
Christian	0	0	34	--	0	491	220	--	10	--	--	--	804
Douglas	0	1	52	--	7	1,555	518	--	6	--	--	--	2,214
Howell	1	4	309	1	4	2,923	1,447	--	13	15	--	7	4,799
McDonald	--	0	47	--	0	654	373	--	67	29	--	17	1,306
Newton	1	0	20	--	0	366	150	--	15	1	--	1	787
Ozark	0	0	16	--	0	572	179	--	21	--	--	--	795
Stone	--	0	24	--	0	331	151	--	12	--	--	0	687
Taney	2	1	11	--	1	279	125	--	8	--	--	0	449
Texas	--	0	197	0	4	3,074	1,144	--	8	0	--	0	4,596
Webster	--	0	16	--	0	203	110	--	0	--	--	--	406
Wright	--	0	23	--	4	546	195	--	1	--	--	--	860
Total	4	8	828	1	22	11,665	4,917	--	184	46	--	27	18,944

Table 7.—Continued

Forest Inventory Unit and county	Cotton-wood	Elm	Hickory	Hard maple	Soft maple	Red oak group	White oak group	Sweet-gum	Syca-more	Tupelo/gum	Yellow-poplar	Other hard-woods	Total hard-woods
Northwestern Ozark Unit													
Benton	0	--	3	--	1	59	51	--	2	--	--	2	181
Camden	1	0	17	3	2	273	307	1	9	--	--	--	663
Cedar	2	0	--	--	--	38	10	--	4	--	--	1	108
Dallas	--	7	42	--	0	227	235	--	13	--	--	--	588
Hickory	--	0	4	--	--	403	220	--	0	--	--	--	717
Laclede	--	0	7	--	1	110	90	--	0	--	--	--	247
Maries	23	6	16	3	24	159	386	--	33	--	--	1	687
Miller	13	0	21	17	14	441	500	8	21	--	--	1	1,104
Morgan	18	--	11	3	3	114	171	1	9	--	--	4	382
Phelps	6	9	78	1	4	811	811	0	68	--	--	1	1,855
Polk	1	--	8	--	0	153	117	--	13	--	--	--	486
Pulaski	--	3	13	--	2	107	116	--	9	--	--	--	314
St. Clair	2	0	14	--	1	79	35	--	2	--	--	1	231
Total	65	25	235	27	51	2,973	3,050	11	184	--	--	10	7,563
Prairie Unit													
Adair	7	2	8	1	20	81	126	--	0	--	--	1	421
Andrew	37	--	--	--	4	5	3	--	4	--	--	0	56
Atchison	4	--	--	0	0	--	1	--	--	--	--	--	20
Audrain	42	1	25	0	16	277	158	--	20	--	--	16	622
Barton	1	0	137	--	71	228	153	--	69	--	--	1	745
Bates	1	1	30	--	1	33	15	--	1	--	--	--	128
Buchanan	--	--	--	--	33	54	36	--	--	--	--	--	228
Caldwell	25	1	3	--	35	12	9	--	3	--	--	3	103
Carroll	169	4	10	--	44	58	25	--	16	--	--	16	354
Cass	0	0	24	--	1	100	93	--	23	--	--	35	283
Chariton	41	5	8	0	31	199	85	--	26	--	--	17	472
Clark	160	9	32	1	28	344	244	--	7	--	--	1	945
Clay	5	1	1	--	1	1	2	--	1	--	--	1	13
Clinton	3	0	0	--	2	4	3	--	1	--	--	0	27
Cooper	48	--	1	0	5	40	53	--	16	--	--	9	236

(Table 7 continued on next page)

Table 7.—Continued

Prairie Unit (cont.)

Dade	1	0	--	--	--	35	20	--	3	--	--	0	130
Daviess	193	21	26	0	60	46	64	--	40	--	--	19	540
De Kalb	25	0	0	--	3	5	4	--	4	--	--	1	56
Gentry	85	0	1	--	4	4	6	--	4	--	--	2	123
Greene	--	1	6	--	0	105	52	--	5	--	--	0	302
Grundy	127	14	19	--	44	38	36	--	24	--	--	14	380
Harrison	112	12	14	--	17	28	26	--	18	--	--	11	312
Henry	3	0	22	--	2	63	61	--	11	--	--	3	191
Holt	18	--	--	--	2	3	3	--	2	--	--	--	35
Jasper	1	0	5	--	3	66	30	--	4	--	--	2	163
Johnson	18	0	6	--	4	30	31	--	20	--	--	2	120
Knox	23	4	14	1	40	85	88	--	4	--	--	1	306
Lafayette	34	1	2	--	2	11	4	--	3	--	--	3	62
Lawrence	--	0	38	--	0	325	170	--	18	--	--	0	766
Lewis	48	8	19	2	39	147	204	--	7	--	--	1	580
Lincoln	85	0	21	3	32	216	164	--	22	--	--	10	591
Linn	6	1	3	0	29	33	23	--	1	--	--	0	123
Livingston	104	3	8	0	25	26	23	--	13	--	--	3	245
Macon	8	3	12	0	13	212	142	--	4	--	--	2	410
Marion	2	2	6	2	3	48	49	--	2	--	--	1	134
Mercer	54	11	12	0	13	23	24	--	12	--	--	12	210
Monroe	16	2	9	0	12	220	109	--	20	--	--	6	429
Nodaway	59	--	0	--	3	3	2	--	4	--	--	1	79
Pettis	19	--	4	1	4	77	79	--	25	--	--	14	369
Pike	94	0	36	3	39	300	78	--	27	--	--	20	651
Putnam	5	--	0	0	14	19	35	--	0	--	--	--	103
Ralls	22	0	24	1	24	226	189	--	8	--	--	14	547
Randolph	47	17	44	1	32	682	488	--	59	--	--	24	1,479
Ray	41	2	3	--	4	11	7	--	5	--	--	4	81
Saline	36	1	2	0	7	22	28	--	7	--	--	5	172
Schuyler	5	1	6	0	41	39	63	--	0	--	--	--	501
Scotland	28	3	11	0	154	135	68	--	3	--	--	0	563
Shelby	3	2	8	0	8	165	50	--	2	--	--	0	249
Sullivan	4	--	0	--	14	11	50	--	--	--	--	--	108
Vernon	2	0	13	--	12	48	20	--	2	--	--	2	242
Worth	26	--	0	--	1	2	3	--	0	--	--	0	40
Total	1,898	134	673	16	996	4,943	3,499	--	571	--	--	279	16,045

Table 7.—Continued

Forest Inventory Unit and county	Cotton-wood	Elm	Hickory	Hard maple	Soft maple	Red oak group	White oak group	Sweet-gum	Syca-more	Tupelo/gum	Yellow-poplar	Other hard-woods	Total hard-woods
Riverborder Unit													
Boone	26	3	18	1	11	182	187	--	32	--	--	3	560
Callaway	1	--	8	2	4	79	182	--	12	--	--	1	342
Cape Girardeau	9	0	74	22	--	325	274	0	0	0	34	1	793
Cole	17	1	9	5	18	155	162	1	18	--	--	1	415
Dunklin	0	1	5	--	1	32	18	5	2	--	--	--	71
Franklin	19	2	28	2	17	230	355	1	21	--	--	1	715
Gasconade	119	2	17	5	28	194	440	1	36	--	--	3	862
Howard	7	1	9	0	7	84	60	--	31	--	--	5	267
Jefferson	1	6	30	7	2	170	176	0	3	--	--	4	423
Mississippi	2	--	0	--	--	--	--	--	--	--	--	--	2
Moniteau	8	--	10	3	2	116	120	1	6	--	--	1	339
Montgomery	78	--	18	4	28	145	122	--	19	--	--	10	454
New Madrid	2	51	2	--	--	9	10	40	1	--	--	341	460
Osage	60	4	17	7	42	323	452	--	39	--	--	7	981
Pemiscot	--	1	--	--	1	--	--	--	--	--	--	--	1
Perry	11	1	114	64	1	1,082	692	2	2	1	235	0	2,459
Scott	2	0	10	4	--	5	18	12	1	--	23	--	76
St. Charles	43	0	9	3	13	23	29	--	9	--	--	0	136
St. Louis	--	--	1	0	1	3	21	--	0	--	--	0	30
Ste. Genevieve	7	--	33	13	--	253	201	1	1	--	24	1	578
Stoddard	7	6	37	0	2	159	166	10	18	--	--	1	418
Warren	72	0	2	4	21	45	165	--	17	--	--	0	349
Total	491	80	441	144	198	3,615	3,852	75	268	1	316	380	10,730
State total	2,529	354	4,749	388	1,374	48,950	27,210	149	1,485	130	397	710	95,125

All table cells without observations are indicated by --. Table value of 0 indicates the volume rounds to less than 1 thousand cubic feet. Columns and rows may not add to their totals due to rounding.

Table 8.—Industrial roundwood production by Forest Inventory Unit, species group, and product, Missouri, 2009

Species group	Total MCF[a]	Saw logs MBF[b]	Saw logs MCF[a]	Veneer logs MBF[b]	Veneer logs MCF[a]	Pulpwood Cords[c]	Pulpwood MCF[a]	Charcoal Cords[c]	Charcoal MCF[a]	Cooperage MBF[b]	Cooperage MCF[a]
				All Units							
Softwoods											
Eastern redcedar	3,214	8,278	2,245	--	--	--	--	--	--	--	--
Cypress	10	58	10	--	--	--	--	--	--	--	--
Shortleaf pine	4,272	17,964	3,120	--	--	3,820	302	--	--	--	--
White pine	2	10	2	--	--	--	--	--	--	--	--
Other pine	2	--	--	--	--	24	2	--	--	--	--
Total	7,499	26,310	5,377	--	--	3,844	304	--	--	--	--
Hardwoods											
Ash	1,284	6,880	1,133	--	--	338	27	--	--	--	--
Basswood	14	82	14	--	--	--	--	--	--	--	--
River birch	46	214	35	--	--	95	8	--	--	--	--
Black cherry	134	687	113	14	3	217	17	1	0	--	--
Black walnut	5,224	22,879	5,008	949	206	107	8	--	--	--	--
cottonwood	2,529	17,584	2,486	--	--	310	24	--	--	--	--
Elm	354	1,711	282	--	--	897	71	--	--	--	--
Hickory	4,749	26,954	4,439	26	6	2,550	201	451	32	--	--
Hard maple	388	2,181	359	33	8	268	21	1	0	--	--
Soft maple	1,374	8,120	1,337	6	1	348	28	--	--	--	--
Red oak group	48,950	267,883	47,683	43	10	11,908	941	1,051	74	--	--
White oak group	27,210	121,820	21,684	2,888	660	11,768	930	189	13	23,054	3,799
Sweetgum	149	700	115	--	--	420	33	--	--	--	--
Sycamore	1,485	8,514	1,402	--	--	467	37	--	--	--	--
Tupelo/gum	130	664	109	--	--	241	19	--	--	--	--
Yellow-poplar	397	2,410	397	--	--	2	0	--	--	--	--
Other hardwoods	710	2,083	343	1	0	4,540	359	1	0	--	--
Total	95,125	491,366	86,941	3,960	894	34,476	2,724	1,694	119	23,054	3,799
State total	102,624	517,676	92,318	3,960	894	38,320	3,027	1,694	119	23,054	3,799

Table 8.—Continued

Species group	Total MCF[a]	Saw logs		Veneer logs		Pulpwood		Charcoal		Cooperage	
		MBF[b]	MCF[a]	MBF[b]	MCF[a]	Cords[c]	MCF[a]	Cords[c]	MCF[a]	MBF[b]	MCF[a]
Softwoods											
Eastern redcedar	409	1,268	344	--	--	--	--	--	--	--	--
Cypress	1	6	1	--	--	--	--	--	--	--	--
Shortleaf pine	2,809	11,912	2,069	--	--	2,435	192	--	--	--	--
Total	3,219	13,186	2,414	--	--	2,435	192	--	--	--	--
Hardwoods											
Ash	311	1,171	193	--	--	32	2	--	--	--	--
River birch	0	--	--	--	--	6	0	--	--	--	--
Black cherry	41	229	38	--	--	37	3	--	--	--	--
Black walnut	270	1,137	249	98	21	--	--	--	--	--	--
Cottonwood	72	506	72	--	--	--	--	--	--	--	--
Elm	107	581	96	--	--	138	11	--	--	--	--
Hickory	2,571	15,069	2,482	8	2	836	66	104	7	--	--
Hard maple	201	1,134	187	--	--	177	14	--	--	--	--
Soft maple	106	626	103	--	--	37	3	--	--	--	--
Red oak group	25,755	143,180	25,486	8	2	2,600	205	832	58	--	--
White oak group	11,892	56,472	10,052	1,279	292	3,581	283	106	7	7,622	1,256
Sweetgum	62	374	62	--	--	3	0	--	--	--	--
Sycamore	278	1,624	267	--	--	130	10	--	--	--	--
Tupelo/gum	83	476	78	--	--	54	4	--	--	--	--
Yellow-poplar	81	492	81	--	--	--	--	--	--	--	--
Other hardwoods	14	43	7	--	--	88	7	--	--	--	--
Total	41,843	223,115	39,452	1,393	317	7,718	610	1,042	73	7,622	1,256
Unit total	45,062	236,302	41,866	1,393	317	10,153	802	1,042	73	7,622	1,256

(Table 8 continued on next page)

Table 8.—Continued

Southwestern Ozark Unit

Softwoods											
Eastern redcedar	820	2,957	802	--	--	--	--	--	--	--	--
Shortleaf pine	1,326	5,473	951	--	--	1,262	100	--	--	--	--
Total	2,146	8,430	1,753	--	--	1,262	100	--	--	--	--
Hardwoods											
Ash	98	559	92	--	--	52	4	--	--	--	--
Black cherry	10	17	3	--	--	89	7	--	--	--	--
Black walnut	1,135	5,066	1,109	122	26	--	--	--	--	--	--
Cottonwood	4	25	4	--	--	--	--	--	--	--	--
Elm	8	32	5	--	--	36	3	--	--	--	--
Hickory	828	3,902	643	1	0	1,458	115	345	24	--	--
Hard maple	1	3	1	--	--	0	0	--	--	--	--
Soft maple	22	134	22	--	--	4	0	--	--	--	--
Red oak group	11,665	60,187	10,713	1	0	8,830	698	220	15	--	70
White oak group	4,917	23,088	4,110	305	70	6,918	546	83	6	427	--
Sycamore	184	884	146	--	--	30	2	--	--	--	--
Tupelo/gum	46	184	30	--	--	187	15	--	--	--	--
Other hardwoods	27	118	19	--	--	92	7	--	--	--	--
Total	18,944	94,199	16,896	430	97	17,697	1,398	647	45	427	70
Unit total	21,090	102,629	18,649	430	97	18,959	1,498	647	45	427	70

Table 8.—Continued

Northwestern Ozark Unit

Species group	Total MCF[a]	Saw logs MBF[b]	Saw logs MCF[a]	Veneer logs MBF[b]	Veneer logs MCF[a]	Pulpwood Cords[c]	Pulpwood MCF[a]	Charcoal Cords[c]	Charcoal MCF[a]	Cooperage MBF[b]	Cooperage MCF[a]
Softwoods											
Eastern redcedar	1,109	2,672	725	--	--	--	--	--	--	--	--
Shortleaf pine	31	116	20	--	--	--	--	--	--	--	--
Total	1,139	2,788	745	--	--	--	--	--	--	--	--
Hardwoods											
Ash	175	1,051	173	--	--	5	0	--	--	--	--
River birch	1	0	0	--	--	--	--	--	--	--	--
Black cherry	1	5	1	--	--	--	--	1	0	--	--
Black walnut	754	3,319	726	124	27	4	0	--	--	--	--
Cottonwood	65	453	64	--	--	--	--	--	--	--	--
Elm	25	154	25	--	--	--	--	--	--	--	--
Hickory	235	1,413	233	2	0	--	--	2	0	--	--
Hard maple	27	162	27	--	--	--	--	1	0	--	--
Soft maple	51	298	49	2	0	1	0	--	--	--	--
Red oak group	2,973	16,700	2,973	--	--	--	--	--	--	--	--
White oak group	3,050	12,831	2,284	189	43	--	--	--	--	4,385	723
Sweetgum	11	68	11	--	--	--	--	--	--	--	--
Sycamore	184	1,096	180	--	--	20	2	--	--	--	--
Other hardwoods	10	46	8	--	--	--	--	1	0	--	--
Total	7,563	37,596	6,754	316	71	30	2	4	0	4,385	723
Unit total	8,702	40,384	7,499	316	71	30	2	4	0	4,385	723

(Table 8 continued on next page)

41

Table 8.—Continued

Prairie Unit

Species											
Softwoods											
Eastern redcedar	87	94	26	---	---	---	---	---	---	---	---
Shortleaf pine	1	4	1	---	---	---	---	---	---	---	---
White pine	1	4	1	---	---	---	---	---	---	---	---
Total	88	102	27	---	---	---	---	---	---	---	---
Hardwoods											
Ash	508	3,045	501	---	---	40	3	---	---	---	---
Basswood	14	82	14	---	---	---	---	---	---	---	---
River birch	35	199	33	---	---	---	---	---	---	---	---
Black cherry	18	101	17	7	2	---	---	0	---	---	---
Black walnut	2,462	10,834	2,371	393	85	60	5	---	---	---	---
Cottonwood	1,898	13,266	1,876	---	---	59	5	---	---	---	---
Elm	134	807	133	---	---	---	---	---	---	---	---
Hickory	673	4,072	671	1	0	---	---	0	0	---	---
Hard maple	16	73	12	17	4	---	---	0	0	---	---
Soft maple	996	5,894	971	6	1	229	18	---	---	---	---
Red oak group	4,943	27,749	4,939	9	2	---	---	---	---	---	---
White oak group	3,499	15,655	2,787	42	9	---	---	---	---	4,220	695
Sycamore	571	3,390	558	---	---	82	7	---	---	---	---
Other hardwoods	279	1,663	274	0	0	---	---	0	0	---	---
Total	16,045	86,829	15,156	474	104	471	37	0	0	4,220	695
Unit total	16,134	86,931	15,183	474	104	471	37	0	0	4,220	695

Table 8.—Continued

Riverborder Unit

Species group	Total MCF[a]	Saw logs MBF[b]	Saw logs MCF[a]	Veneer logs MBF[b]	Veneer logs MCF[a]	Pulpwood Cords[c]	Pulpwood MCF[a]	Charcoal Cords[c]	Charcoal MCF[a]	Cooperage MBF[b]	Cooperage MCF[a]
Softwoods											
Eastern redcedar	789	1,287	349	--	--	--	--	--	--	--	--
Cypress	9	52	9	--	--	--	--	--	--	--	--
Shortleaf pine	105	459	80	--	--	123	10	--	--	--	--
White pine	1	6	1	--	--	--	--	--	--	--	--
Other pine	2	--	--	--	--	24	2	--	--	--	--
Total	906	1,804	439	--	--	147	12	--	--	--	--
Hardwoods											
Ash	193	1,055	174	--	--	209	17	--	--	--	--
River birch	9	14	2	--	--	89	7	--	--	--	--
Black cherry	64	336	55	7	2	91	7	0	0	--	--
Black walnut	602	2,524	552	212	46	43	3	--	--	--	--
Cottonwood	491	3,334	471	--	--	251	20	--	--	--	--
Elm	80	136	22	--	--	722	57	--	--	--	--
Hickory	441	2,498	411	14	3	257	20	0	0	--	--
Hard maple	144	809	133	17	4	91	7	0	0	--	--
Soft maple	198	1,168	192	--	--	77	6	--	--	--	--
Red oak group	3,615	20,067	3,572	23	5	477	38	--	--	--	--
White oak group	3,852	13,774	2,452	1,074	246	1,270	100	--	--	6,400	1,055
Sweetgum	75	257	42	--	--	417	33	--	--	--	--
Sycamore	268	1,521	250	--	--	204	16	--	--	--	--
Tupelo/gum	1	4	1	--	--	0	0	--	--	--	--
Yellow-poplar	316	1,918	316	--	--	2	0	--	--	--	--
Other hardwoods	380	213	35	0	0	4,359	344	0	0	--	--
Total	10,730	49,627	8,683	306	306	8,560	676	0	0	6,400	1,055
Unit total	11,636	51,431	9,122	306	306	8,707	688	0	0	6,400	1,055

(Table 8 continued on next page)

Table 8.—Continued

Species group	Handles		Industrial fuelwood		Poles		Posts		Excelsior/ shavings	Cabin logs
	MBF[b]	MCF[a]	Cords[c]	MCF[a]	Pieces	MCF[a]	Mpieces[d]	MCF[a]	MCF[a]	MCF[a]
				All Units						
Softwoods										
Eastern redcedar	--	--	--	--	13,044	39	7	5	--	924
Cypress	--	--	--	--	--	--	--	--	--	--
Shortleaf pine	--	--	300	21	168,920	507	297	229	--	93
White pine	--	--	--	--	--	--	--	--	--	--
Other pine	--	--	--	--	--	--	--	--	--	--
Total	--	--	300	21	181,964	546	304	234	--	1,017
Hardwoods										
Ash	743	120	--	--	309	1	--	--	--	4
Basswood	--	--	--	--	--	--	--	--	--	--
River birch	--	--	--	--	--	--	--	--	--	4
Black cherry	--	--	--	--	--	--	--	--	--	--
Black walnut	--	--	--	--	273	1	--	--	--	--
cottonwood	--	--	120	8	1,636	6	--	--	--	4
Elm	--	--	--	--	309	1	--	--	--	--
Hickory	149	24	600	42	1,085	4	--	--	--	--
Hard maple	--	--	--	--	36	0	--	--	--	--
Soft maple	--	--	15	1	273	1	--	--	--	6
Red oak group	--	--	1,200	84	993	4	2	1	--	154
White oak group	--	--	900	63	1,996	8	1	0	1	51
Sweetgum	--	--	--	--	36	0	--	--	--	--
Sycamore	--	--	15	1	309	1	--	--	--	43
Tupelo/gum	--	--	--	--	--	--	--	--	--	1
Yellow-poplar	1	0	--	--	--	--	--	--	--	--
Other hardwoods	--	--	--	--	--	--	--	--	0	7
Total	893	144	2,850	200	7,254	28	2	1	1	274
State total	893	144	3,150	221	189,218	574	307	236	1	1,291

Table 8.—Continued

Species group	Handles		Industrial fuelwood		Poles		Posts		Excelsior/ shavings	Cabin logs
	MBF[b]	MCF[a]	Cords[c]	MCF[a]	Pieces	MCF[a]	Mpieces[d]	MCF[a]	MCF[a]	MCF[a]

Eastern Ozark Unit

Species group	MBF[b]	MCF[a]	Cords[c]	MCF[a]	Pieces	MCF[a]	Mpieces[d]	MCF[a]	MCF[a]	MCF[a]
Softwoods										
Eastern redcedar	--	--	--	--	9,783	29	0	0	--	36
Cypress	--	--	--	--	--	--	--	--	--	--
Shortleaf pine	--	--	--	--	124,744	374	169	130	--	43
Total	--	--	--	--	134,527	404	169	130	--	79
Hardwoods										
Ash	715	115	--	--	36	0	--	--	--	--
River birch	--	--	--	--	--	--	--	--	--	--
Black cherry	--	--	--	--	--	--	--	--	--	--
Black walnut	--	--	--	--	--	--	--	--	--	--
Cottonwood	--	--	--	--	--	--	--	--	--	--
Elm	--	--	--	--	36	0	--	--	--	--
Hickory	75	12	--	--	540	2	--	--	--	--
Hard maple	--	--	--	--	36	0	--	--	--	--
Soft maple	--	--	--	--	--	--	--	--	--	--
Red oak group	--	--	--	--	720	3	1	0	--	--
White oak group	--	--	--	--	360	1	--	--	--	--
Sweetgum	--	--	--	--	36	0	--	--	--	--
Sycamore	--	--	--	--	36	0	--	--	--	--
Tupelo/gum	--	--	--	--	--	--	--	--	--	--
Yellow-poplar	--	--	--	--	--	--	--	--	--	--
Other hardwoods	--	--	--	--	--	--	--	--	--	--
Total	790	127	--	--	1,800	7	--	--	--	--
Unit total	790	127	--	--	136,327	411	169	130	--	79

(Table 8 continued on next page)

45

Table 8.—Continued

Southwestern Ozark Unit

Softwoods											
Eastern redcedar	--	--	--	--	3,261	--	10	6	5	--	4
Shortleaf pine	--	--	300	21	42,741	--	128	115	89	--	37
Total	--	--	300	21	46,002	--	138	122	94	--	41
Hardwoods											
Ash	1	8	--	--	--	--	--	--	--	--	--
Black cherry	--	--	--	--	--	--	--	--	--	--	--
Black walnut	--	--	--	--	--	--	--	--	--	--	--
Cottonwood	--	--	--	--	--	--	--	--	--	--	--
Elm	--	--	--	--	--	--	--	--	--	--	--
Hickory	4	24	600	42	--	--	--	--	--	--	--
Hard maple	--	--	--	--	--	--	--	--	--	--	--
Soft maple	--	--	--	--	--	--	--	--	--	--	--
Red oak group	--	--	1,200	84	--	--	--	1	0	--	154
White oak group	--	--	900	63	--	--	--	0	0	--	51
Sycamore	--	--	--	--	--	--	--	--	--	--	36
Tupelo/gum	--	--	--	--	--	--	--	--	--	--	1
Other hardwoods	--	--	--	--	--	--	--	--	--	--	--
Total	5	32	2,700	189	--	--	--	1	1	--	243
Unit total	5	32	3,000	210	46,002	--	138	123	94	--	284

46

Table 8.—Continued

Northwestern Ozark Unit

Species group	Handles		Industrial fuelwood		Poles		Posts		Excelsior/ shavings	Cabin logs
	MBF[b]	MCF[a]	Cords[c]	MCF[a]	Pieces	MCF[a]	Mpieces[d]	MCF[a]	MCF[a]	MCF[a]
Softwoods										
Eastern redcedar	--	--	--	--	--	--	--	--	--	384
Shortleaf pine	--	--	--	--	--	--	12	9	--	1
Total	--	--	--	--	--	--	12	9	--	385
Hardwoods										
Ash	3	1	--	--	--	--	--	--	--	1
River birch	--	--	--	--	--	--	--	--	--	1
Black cherry	--	--	--	--	--	--	--	--	--	--
Black walnut	--	--	--	--	--	--	--	--	--	1
Cottonwood	--	--	--	--	--	--	--	--	--	1
Elm	--	--	--	--	--	--	--	--	--	--
Hickory	10	2	--	--	--	--	--	--	--	--
Hard maple	--	--	--	--	--	--	--	--	--	--
Soft maple	--	--	--	--	--	--	--	--	--	2
Red oak group	--	--	--	--	--	--	0	0	--	1
White oak group	--	--	--	--	--	--	--	--	--	--
Sweetgum	--	--	--	--	--	--	--	--	--	2
Sycamore	--	--	--	--	--	--	--	--	--	2
Other hardwoods	--	--	--	--	--	--	--	--	--	2
Total	14	2	--	--	--	--	0	0	--	10
Unit total	14	2	--	--	--	--	12	9	--	395

(Table 8 continued on next page)

47

Table 8.—Continued

Prairie Unit

Softwoods						
Eastern redcedar	61	--	--	--	--	--
Shortleaf pine	0	--	--	--	--	--
White pine	--	--	--	--	--	--
Total	62	--	--	--	--	--
Hardwoods						
Ash	2	--	1	273	--	--
Basswood	--	--	--	--	--	--
River birch	2	--	--	--	--	--
Black cherry	--	--	--	--	--	--
Black walnut	--	--	1	273	--	--
Cottonwood	2	--	6	1,636	8	120
Elm	--	--	1	273	--	--
Hickory	--	--	2	545	--	--
Hard maple	--	--	--	--	--	--
Soft maple	4	--	1	273	1	15
Red oak group	--	0	1	273	--	--
White oak group	--	0	6	1,636	--	--
Sycamore	4	--	1	273	1	15
Other hardwoods	5	0	--	--	--	--
Total	19	1	21	5,454	11	150
Unit total	81	1	21	5,454	11	150

Table 8.—Continued

Riverborder Unit

Species group	Handles		Industrial fuelwood		Poles		Posts		Excelsior/ shavings	Cabin logs
	MBF[b]	MCF[a]	Cords[c]	MCF[a]	Pieces	MCF[a]	Mpieces[d]	MCF[a]	MCF[a]	MCF[a]
Softwoods										
Eastern redcedar	--	--	--	--	--	--	1	1	--	439
Cypress	--	--	--	--	--	--	--	--	--	--
Shortleaf pine	--	--	--	--	1,435	4	1	1	--	11
White pine	--	--	--	--	--	--	--	--	--	--
Other pine	--	--	--	--	--	--	--	--	--	--
Total	--	--	--	--	1,435	4	2	1	--	450
Hardwoods										
Ash	17	3	--	--	--	--	--	--	--	--
River birch	--	--	--	--	--	--	--	--	--	--
Black cherry	--	--	--	--	--	--	--	--	--	--
Black walnut	--	--	--	--	--	--	--	--	--	--
Cottonwood	--	--	--	--	--	--	--	--	--	--
Elm	--	--	--	--	--	--	--	--	--	--
Hickory	39	6	--	--	--	--	--	--	--	--
Hard maple	--	--	--	--	--	--	--	--	--	--
Soft maple	--	--	--	--	--	--	--	--	--	--
Red oak group	--	--	--	--	--	--	0	0	--	--
White oak group	--	--	--	--	--	--	--	--	--	--
Sweetgum	--	--	--	--	--	--	--	--	--	--
Sycamore	--	--	--	--	--	--	--	--	--	1
Tupelo/gum	--	--	--	--	--	--	--	--	--	--
Yellow-poplar	1	0	--	--	--	--	--	--	--	--
Other hardwoods	--	--	--	--	--	--	--	--	--	--
Total	57	9	--	--	--	--	0	0	--	1
Unit total	57	9	--	--	1,435	4	2	2	--	451

All table cells without observations are indicated by --. Table value of 0 indicates the volume rounds to less than 1 unit of measure. Columns and rows may not add to their totals due to rounding.

[a] Thousand cubic feet.
[b] Thousand board feet, International ¼-inch rule.
[c] Standard cords are 128 cubic feet consisting of 79 cubic feet of wood and 49 cubic feet of bark and air space.
[d] Thousand pieces.

Table 9.—Saw log receipts and production, in thousand board feet[a], by Forest Inventory Unit and species group, Missouri, 2006 and 2009

All Units

Species group	Receipts			Production		
	2006	2009	Percent change	2006	2009	Percent change
Softwoods						
Eastern redcedar	9,203	9,363	2%	9,002	8,278	-8%
Cypress	122	58	-52%	121	58	-52%
Shortleaf pine	18,358	14,971	-18%	18,924	17,964	-5%
White pine	0	24	>1,000%[b]	0	10	>1,000%[b]
Total	27,683	24,417	-12%	28,047	26,310	-6%
Hardwoods						
Ash	9,136	7,060	-23%	8,237	6,880	-16%
Basswood	75	2	-97%	119	82	-31%
River birch	297	214	-28%	297	214	-28%
Black cherry	1,503	843	-44%	812	687	-15%
Black walnut	18,449	24,887	35%	25,656	22,879	-11%
Cottonwood	22,150	18,447	-17%	19,751	17,584	-11%
Elm	3,017	1,667	-45%	2,852	1,711	-40%
Hickory	38,236	28,478	-26%	35,804	26,954	-25%
Hard maple	3,168	2,560	-19%	2,890	2,181	-25%
Soft maple	13,233	9,204	-30%	11,809	8,120	-31%
Red oak group	327,928	277,906	-15%	312,330	267,883	-14%
White oak group	163,529	125,385	-23%	152,457	121,820	-20%
Sweetgum	2,003	595	-70%	1,940	700	-64%
Sycamore	12,965	8,737	-33%	11,092	8,514	-23%
Tupelo/gum	570	673	18%	625	664	6%
Yellow-poplar	2,526	3,681	46%	1,241	2,410	94%
Other hardwoods	2,297	2,054	-11%	2,363	2,083	-12%
Total	621,081	512,393	-17%	590,273	491,366	-17%
State total	648,764	536,810	-17%	618,321	517,676	-16%

Table 9.—Continued

Eastern Ozark Unit

Species group	Receipts			Production		
	2006	2009	Percent change	2006	2009	Percent change
Softwoods						
Eastern redcedar	1,097	1,354	24%	661	1,268	92%
Cypress	80	10	-87%	80	6	-93%
Shortleaf pine	14,666	12,516	-15%	15,515	11,912	-23%
White pine	--	--	--	--	--	--
Total	15,842	13,881	-12%	16,256	13,186	-19%
Hardwoods						
Ash	1,911	944	-51%	1,537	1,171	-24%
Basswood	--	--	--	--	--	--
River birch	--	--	--	--	--	--
Black cherry	109	90	-18%	122	229	88%
Black walnut	475	249	-48%	677	1,137	68%
Cottonwood	1,045	408	-61%	776	506	-35%
Elm	1,143	601	-47%	811	581	-28%
Hickory	23,130	16,097	-30%	20,676	15,069	-27%
Hard maple	1,114	971	-13%	850	1,134	33%
Soft maple	1,468	637	-57%	895	626	-30%
Red oak group	176,747	140,536	-20%	172,329	143,180	-17%
White oak group	70,738	58,653	-17%	63,201	56,472	-11%
Sweetgum	1,286	422	-67%	1,127	374	-67%
Sycamore	2,020	1,668	-17%	1,514	1,624	7%
Tupelo/gum	330	480	45%	150	476	217%
Yellow-poplar	331	--	--	163	492	203%
Other hardwoods	3	54	>1,000%[b]	3	43	>1,000%[b]
Total	281,849	221,811	-21%	264,829	223,115	-16%
Unit total	297,691	235,692	-21%	281,085	236,302	-16%

(Table 9 continued on next page)

51

Table 9.—Continued

Southwestern Ozark Unit

Softwoods						
Eastern redcedar	5,101	-24%	3,890	4,946	-40%	2,957
Cypress	—	—	—	—	—	—
Shortleaf pine	2,530	-24%	1,931	2,709	102%	5,473
White pine	—	—	—	—	—	—
Total	7,631	-24%	5,821	7,655	10%	8,430
Hardwoods						
Ash	223	3%	230	895	-38%	559
Basswood	—	—	—	—	—	—
River birch	—	—	—	—	—	—
Black cherry	1,000	-99%	13	300	-94%	17
Black walnut	6,516	127%	14,764	6,414	-21%	5,066
Cottonwood	17	—	17	150	-83%	25
Elm	12	17%	13	57	-43%	32
Hickory	3,569	4%	3,713	4,483	-13%	3,902
Hard maple	25	—	—	154	-98%	3
Soft maple	48	261%	173	97	39%	134
Red oak group	63,385	9%	69,157	55,860	8%	60,187
White oak group	25,265	-6%	23,662	21,770	6%	23,088
Sweetgum	—	—	—	127	—	—
Sycamore	2,042	-62%	786	1,187	-26%	884
Tupelo/gum	240	-20%	193	244	-25%	184
Yellow-poplar	—	—	—	16	—	—
Other hardwoods	132	-11%	118	368	-68%	118
Total	102,458	10%	112,840	92,120	2%	94,199
Unit total	110,089	8%	118,661	99,775	3%	102,629

Table 9.—Continued

Northwestern Ozark Unit

Species group	Receipts			Production		
	2006	2009	Percent change	2006	2009	Percent change
Softwoods						
Eastern redcedar	1,205	2,817	134%	1,208	2,672	121%
Cypress	--	--	--	--	--	--
Shortleaf pine	--	--	--	362	116	-68%
White pine	--	--	--	--	--	--
Total	1,205	2,817	134%	1,570	2,788	78%
Hardwoods						
Ash	419	1,143	173%	324	1,051	224%
Basswood	--	--	--	--	--	--
River birch	--	--	--	--	0	--
Black cherry	3	3	-17%	7	5	-31%
Black walnut	1,219	1,294	6%	2,139	3,319	55%
Cottonwood	138	135	-2%	336	453	35%
Elm	40	141	253%	52	154	196%
Hickory	2,158	1,167	-46%	1,659	1,413	-15%
Hard maple	25	166	567%	6	162	2733%
Soft maple	158	83	-48%	251	298	19%
Red oak group	18,127	14,088	-22%	24,761	16,700	-33%
White oak group	18,427	11,609	-37%	22,150	12,831	-42%
Sweetgum	--	83	--	--	68	--
Sycamore	1,160	928	-20%	1,120	1,096	-2%
Tupelo/gum	--	--	--	--	--	--
Yellow-poplar	--	--	--	--	--	--
Other hardwoods	9	--	--	24	46	96%
Total	41,882	30,839	-26%	52,829	37,596	-29%
Unit total	43,087	33,656	-22%	54,399	40,384	-26%

(Table 9 continued on next page)

53

Table 9.—Continued

Softwoods						
Eastern redcedar	116	-62%	43	106	94	-11%
Cypress	1	--	--	--	--	--
Shortleaf pine	--	--	--	--	4	--
White pine	--	--	--	--	4	--
Total	116	-63%	43	106	102	-3%
Hardwoods						
Ash	4,339	-24%	3,280	3,850	3,045	-21%
Basswood	75	-97%	2	117	82	-30%
River birch	297	-28%	214	263	199	-24%
Black cherry	134	-74%	35	216	101	-53%
Black walnut	6,403	-9%	5,814	14,327	10,834	-24%
Cottonwood	18,808	-16%	15,710	14,672	13,266	-10%
Elm	1,821	-56%	806	1,715	807	-53%
Hickory	5,937	-20%	4,759	5,262	4,072	-23%
Hard maple	1,035	-85%	153	336	73	-78%
Soft maple	10,414	-28%	7,494	9,125	5,894	-35%
Red oak group	39,355	-18%	32,333	33,756	27,749	-18%
White oak group	31,232	-44%	17,557	25,109	15,655	-38%
Sweetgum	55	--	--	36	--	--
Sycamore	6,171	-29%	4,393	4,990	3,390	-32%
Tupelo/gum	--	--	--	--	--	--
Yellow-poplar	--	--	--	--	--	--
Other hardwoods	2,111	-16%	1,779	1,807	1,663	-8%
Total	128,187	-26%	94,330	115,582	86,829	-25%
Unit total	128,303	-26%	94,374	115,687	86,931	-25%

Table 9.—Continued

Riverborder Unit

Species group	Receipts			Production		
	2006	2009	Percent change	2006	2009	Percent change
Softwoods						
Eastern redcedar	1,685	1,257	-25%	2,080	1,287	-38%
Cypress	41	48	17%	41	52	27%
Shortleaf pine	1,162	524	-55%	339	459	35%
White pine	0	24	>1,000%[b]	0	6	>1,000%[b]
Total	2,889	1,854	-36%	2,461	1,804	-27%
Hardwoods						
Ash	2,244	1,463	-35%	1,630	1,055	-35%
Basswood	--	--	--	1	--	--
River birch	--	--	--	33	14	-57%
Black cherry	257	703	173%	167	336	101%
Black walnut	3,835	2,767	-28%	2,099	2,524	20%
Cottonwood	2,159	2,177	1%	3,816	3,334	-13%
Elm	1	105	>1,000%[b]	218	136	-37%
Hickory	3,442	2,742	-20%	3,723	2,498	-33%
Hard maple	970	1,270	31%	1,544	809	-48%
Soft maple	1,145	816	-29%	1,442	1,168	-19%
Red oak group	30,314	21,791	-28%	25,625	20,067	-22%
White oak group	17,866	13,905	-22%	20,227	13,774	-32%
Sweetgum	662	90	-86%	651	257	-60%
Sycamore	1,572	962	-39%	2,281	1,521	-33%
Tupelo/gum	--	--	--	232	4	-98%
Yellow-poplar	2,196	3,681	68%	1,063	1,918	80%
Other hardwoods	43	103	139%	163	213	31%
Total	66,705	52,574	-21%	64,914	49,627	-24%
Unit total	69,594	54,428	-22%	67,375	51,431	-24%

All table cells without observations are indicated by -- . Table value of 0 indicates the volume rounds to less than 1 thousand board feet. Columns and rows may not add to their totals due to rounding.

[a] Thousand board feet, International ¼-inch rule.

[b] Volumes are too small to calculate a meaningful percent change.

55

Table 10.—Wood material harvested for industrial roundwood, in thousand cubic feet, by Forest Inventory Unit, source of material, and species group, Missouri, 2009[a]

All Units

	Source of material													
	Growing stock				Non-growing stock									
	Used for products		Logging residue (not used)	Total growing stock	Used for products					Logging slash (not used)	Total non-growing stock	Total wood material used	Total wood material not used	Total wood material harvested
Species group	Saw-timber	Pole-timber			Limb-wood	Sap-lings	Cull trees	Dead trees	Non-forest trees					
Softwoods														
Eastern redcedar	1,431.3	1,273.2	323.2	3,027.7	116.7	9.7	377.5	5.3	--	1,575.7	2,084.9	3,213.7	1,898.9	5,112.6
Cypress	9.8	0.1	1.3	11.1	0.2	--	0.1	--	--	5.7	6.0	10.1	7.0	17.1
Shortleaf pine	3,391.5	704.2	401.7	4,497.4	58.6	60.1	43.5	12.2	1.3	1,865.0	2,040.7	4,271.5	2,266.7	6,538.2
White pine	1.6	0.0	0.2	1.8	0.0	--	0.0	--	--	0.9	1.0	1.7	1.2	2.8
Other pine	0.5	1.4	0.0	1.9	--	--	0.0	--	--	0.2	0.2	1.9	0.2	2.1
Total	4,834.7	1,978.9	726.4	7,540.0	175.6	69.8	421.1	17.5	1.3	3,447.5	4,132.8	7,498.9	4,173.9	11,672.8
Hardwoods														
Ash	958.6	51.2	444.9	1,454.7	15.9	0.3	92.2	0.2	165.8	982.2	1,256.7	1,284.3	1,427.1	2,711.4
Basswood	10.2	0.2	4.2	14.7	0.1	--	0.9	--	2.0	11.6	14.6	13.5	15.8	29.3
River birch	31.3	5.5	11.4	48.2	1.3	0.3	2.6	0.1	5.2	30.9	40.4	46.3	42.3	88.6
Black cherry	99.7	2.6	36.3	138.6	4.1	0.0	10.4	0.1	16.6	98.5	129.7	133.5	134.7	268.3
Black walnut	2,169.6	6.5	323.2	2,499.4	1.0	0.4	2,228.9	0.1	817.0	1,148.6	4,196.0	5,223.6	1,471.8	6,695.4
Cottonwood	2,269.3	24.2	403.2	2,696.7	189.9	1.1	43.8	0.4	0.5	1,338.9	1,574.6	2,529.2	1,742.1	4,271.3
Elm	257.9	8.8	91.2	357.8	15.1	--	30.5	0.4	41.2	246.9	334.1	353.9	338.1	692.0
Hickory	3,525.4	107.3	1,415.4	5,048.1	84.5	0.3	375.3	1.5	654.2	3,828.2	4,944.1	4,748.6	5,243.6	9,992.2
Hard maple	293.3	7.1	113.7	414.2	7.4	0.0	27.7	0.1	52.6	310.1	397.8	388.1	423.9	812.0
Soft maple	1,028.0	39.8	419.3	1,487.1	17.5	1.0	91.8	0.4	195.8	1,149.7	1,456.1	1,374.2	1,569.0	2,943.2
Red oak group	39,890.0	1,158.3	10,016.9	51,065.3	840.2	0.7	6,107.0	944.0	10.0	24,943.4	32,845.4	48,950.3	34,960.4	83,910.7
White oak group	22,528.7	551.7	5,551.0	28,631.3	482.6	0.3	3,209.2	432.5	4.8	11,634.6	15,764.1	27,209.8	17,185.5	44,395.3
Sweetgum	108.1	3.4	37.3	148.8	6.9	--	13.1	0.2	16.9	101.2	138.3	148.6	138.6	287.2
Sycamore	1,115.8	44.8	443.3	1,603.9	19.8	1.0	97.7	0.4	205.2	1,208.4	1,532.6	1,484.8	1,651.7	3,136.5
Tupelo/gum	96.0	2.7	35.0	133.7	4.4	--	10.5	0.1	16.0	95.2	126.2	129.7	130.2	259.9
Yellow-poplar	301.4	6.8	124.2	432.4	4.1	--	26.8	0.0	58.1	340.5	429.5	397.2	464.8	861.9
Other hardwoods	489.9	20.6	121.7	632.1	65.3	0.0	81.3	2.3	50.3	320.2	519.4	709.6	441.9	1,151.5
Total	75,173.2	2,041.5	19,592.4	96,807.1	1,760.1	5.5	12,449.8	1,382.9	2,312.2	47,789.1	65,699.6	95,125.2	67,381.5	162,506.7
State total	80,007.9	4,020.5	20,318.8	104,347.2	1,935.7	75.3	12,870.9	1,400.4	2,313.5	51,236.6	69,832.4	102,624.1	71,555.4	174,179.5

Table 10.—Continued

Eastern Ozark Unit

Species group	Growing stock				Non-growing stock							Total wood material used	Total wood material not used	Total wood material harvested
	Used for products		Logging residue (not used)	Total growing stock	Used for products					Logging slash (not used)	Total non-growing stock			
	Saw-timber	Pole-timber			Limb-wood	Sap-lings	Cull trees	Dead trees	Non-forest trees					
Softwoods														
Eastern redcedar	130.5	200.6	39.9	371.0	17.9	1.3	57.8	0.8	--	236.7	314.5	408.9	276.6	685.5
Cypress	1.0	0.0	0.1	1.1	0.0	--	0.0	--	--	0.6	0.6	1.0	0.7	1.7
Shortleaf pine	2,237.1	472.0	264.6	2,973.8	38.1	34.1	20.8	6.9	--	1,236.2	1,336.1	2,809.1	1,500.8	4,309.9
Total	2,368.6	672.6	304.6	3,345.9	56.0	35.3	78.7	7.7	--	1,473.5	1,651.2	3,219.0	1,778.2	4,997.1
Hardwoods														
Ash	227.3	27.1	146.2	400.7	2.4	--	25.6	0.0	28.2	173.2	229.5	310.6	319.5	630.1
River birch	0.3	0.0	0.0	0.3	0.1	--	0.1	0.0	--	0.0	0.2	0.5	0.0	0.5
Black cherry	30.4	0.8	11.9	43.0	0.9	--	3.0	0.0	5.5	32.5	41.9	40.5	44.4	84.9
Black walnut	112.6	--	16.8	129.4	--	--	115.3	--	42.2	57.4	214.9	270.1	74.2	344.3
Cottonwood	65.1	--	11.5	76.6	5.4	--	1.1	--	--	38.5	45.0	71.6	50.0	121.6
Elm	79.4	2.2	30.4	112.0	2.9	--	8.2	0.1	14.0	82.9	108.1	106.8	113.3	220.1
Hickory	1,935.7	50.8	788.4	2,774.9	37.4	0.0	183.3	0.4	363.6	2,135.5	2,720.3	2,571.3	2,923.9	5,495.2
Hard maple	150.4	3.9	59.0	213.2	4.3	--	14.8	0.1	27.3	161.2	207.8	200.8	220.2	421.0
Soft maple	80.1	1.9	32.4	114.3	1.6	--	7.4	0.0	15.1	88.7	112.8	106.1	121.0	227.1
Red oak group	21,054.9	595.4	5,335.1	26,985.4	396.5	0.3	3,201.4	502.6	3.7	13,305.7	17,410.1	25,754.7	18,640.8	44,395.5
White oak group	9,855.7	239.9	2,440.7	12,536.4	194.9	0.0	1,401.8	199.5	0.5	5,351.3	7,147.9	11,892.3	7,792.0	19,684.3
Sweetgum	47.0	1.2	19.3	67.5	0.7	--	4.2	0.0	9.0	52.9	66.8	62.1	72.3	134.4
Sycamore	209.4	5.1	84.1	298.5	4.5	--	19.7	0.1	39.1	230.2	293.6	277.9	314.3	592.2
Tupelo/gum	62.2	1.5	24.7	88.4	1.5	--	6.0	0.0	11.5	67.6	86.6	82.7	92.3	175.0
Yellow-poplar	61.5	1.4	25.3	88.2	0.8	--	5.5	--	11.9	69.5	87.7	81.0	94.9	175.9
Other hardwoods	9.7	0.4	2.5	12.6	1.3	--	1.6	0.0	1.0	6.6	10.6	14.1	9.1	23.2
Total	33,981.6	931.5	9,028.3	43,941.5	655.1	0.3	4,999.0	702.9	572.7	21,853.8	28,783.8	41,843.1	30,882.1	72,725.2
Unit total	36,350.2	1,604.1	9,333.0	47,287.4	711.1	35.7	5,077.7	710.5	572.7	23,327.3	30,435.0	45,062.1	32,660.3	77,722.4

(Table 10 continued on next page)

Table 10.—Continued

Southwestern Ozark Unit

Softwoods														
Eastern redcedar	213.9	423.7	85.8	723.4	41.7	4.2	134.8	2.0	--	541.3	724.1	820.4	627.1	1,447.5
Shortleaf pine	1,040.4	215.5	123.3	1,379.2	18.7	23.4	21.6	4.8	1.3	569.0	638.7	1,325.6	692.3	2,017.9
Total	1,254.3	639.3	209.1	2,102.6	60.3	27.6	156.4	6.8	1.3	1,110.3	1,362.8	2,146.0	1,319.4	3,465.4
Hardwoods														
Ash	73.4	2.0	29.9	105.3	1.7	--	7.0	0.0	13.5	79.4	101.6	97.5	109.3	206.9
Black cherry	6.4	0.3	1.1	7.9	1.2	--	1.3	0.0	0.4	2.8	5.8	9.8	3.9	13.7
Black walnut	471.7	--	70.2	541.9	--	--	485.6	--	178.1	253.6	917.4	1,135.5	323.8	1,459.3
Cottonwood	3.2	--	0.6	3.8	0.3	--	0.1	--	--	1.9	2.2	3.5	2.5	6.0
Elm	5.8	0.2	1.8	7.8	0.5	--	0.8	0.0	0.8	4.8	7.0	8.2	6.6	14.8
Hickory	569.9	29.6	208.2	807.7	30.0	0.3	99.2	0.9	98.2	562.4	791.0	828.1	770.6	1,598.7
Hard maple	0.4	0.0	0.2	0.6	0.0	--	0.0	0.0	0.1	0.5	0.6	0.6	0.6	1.2
Soft maple	17.0	0.4	6.9	24.3	0.3	--	1.5	0.0	3.2	19.0	24.1	22.5	26.0	48.4
Red oak group	9,378.1	302.2	2,279.5	11,959.8	276.0	0.4	1,486.5	215.4	6.3	5,647.4	7,631.9	11,664.9	7,926.8	19,591.8
White oak group	3,900.5	132.4	906.9	4,939.8	155.8	0.3	639.0	84.5	4.4	2,194.9	3,078.8	4,916.7	3,101.8	8,018.6
Sycamore	144.8	5.9	48.9	199.5	1.9	--	10.2	0.0	21.3	127.4	160.8	184.1	176.3	360.3
Tupelo/gum	33.3	1.2	10.1	44.6	2.9	--	4.4	0.1	4.4	27.0	38.9	46.3	37.2	83.5
Other hardwoods	19.3	0.6	6.4	26.3	1.5	--	2.5	0.0	2.8	17.2	24.0	26.7	23.6	50.3
Total	14,623.8	474.8	3,570.7	18,669.3	472.0	1.0	2,738.3	301.0	333.5	8,938.3	12,784.1	18,944.4	12,509.0	31,453.4
Unit total	15,878.1	1,114.0	3,779.8	20,771.9	532.4	28.6	2,894.7	307.8	334.8	10,048.6	14,146.9	21,090.5	13,828.4	34,918.8

Table 10.—Continued

Northwestern Ozark Unit

| | Growing stock | | | | Non-growing stock | | | | | | | | | |
| | Used for products | | Logging residue (not used) | Total growing stock | Used for products | | | | | Logging slash (not used) | Total non-growing stock | Total wood material used | Total wood material not used | Total wood material harvested |
Species group	Saw-timber	Pole-timber			Limb-wood	Sap-lings	Cull trees	Dead trees	Non-forest trees					
Softwoods														
Eastern redcedar	535.3	409.5	112.1	1,056.9	37.7	2.7	121.8	1.6	--	512.8	676.6	1,108.5	624.9	1,733.4
Shortleaf pine	22.5	4.8	2.6	29.8	0.4	2.5	0.2	0.5	--	12.3	15.9	30.8	14.9	45.7
Total	557.7	414.3	114.7	1,086.7	38.0	5.1	122.0	2.1	--	525.1	692.4	1,139.3	639.8	1,779.1
Hardwoods														
Ash	132.9	3.4	54.6	191.0	1.8	0.0	11.7	0.0	25.3	148.6	187.5	175.2	203.2	378.5
River birch	1.2	0.1	0.1	1.4	0.0	--	0.0	--	0.0	0.1	0.2	1.3	0.3	1.6
Black cherry	0.6	0.0	0.3	0.9	0.0	0.0	0.1	0.0	0.1	0.7	0.9	0.9	1.0	1.8
Black walnut	313.3	0.2	46.6	360.1	0.0	0.0	322.1	0.0	118.1	166.4	606.6	753.6	213.1	966.7
Cottonwood	59.4	0.1	10.4	69.9	4.8	--	1.0	--	--	34.5	40.3	65.3	44.9	110.2
Elm	19.3	0.4	7.9	27.6	0.3	--	1.7	--	3.7	21.8	27.5	25.4	29.7	55.1
Hickory	178.2	4.3	74.1	256.6	2.4	0.0	15.9	0.0	34.1	199.8	252.2	234.9	273.9	508.8
Hard maple	20.3	0.5	8.3	29.1	0.3	0.0	1.8	0.0	3.9	22.9	28.9	26.7	31.2	58.0
Soft maple	39.1	1.1	15.5	55.7	0.5	0.0	3.3	0.0	7.2	42.2	53.2	51.2	57.8	109.0
Red oak group	2,440.3	66.8	621.3	3,128.3	41.8	0.0	365.7	58.5	0.0	1,549.8	2,015.7	2,973.0	2,171.1	5,144.1
White oak group	2,571.5	51.3	656.6	3,279.4	34.7	--	347.2	44.9	--	1,234.1	1,660.9	3,049.6	1,890.6	4,940.2
Sweetgum	8.5	0.2	3.5	12.2	0.1	--	0.8	--	1.6	9.6	12.2	11.2	13.2	24.4
Sycamore	139.1	4.3	56.6	200.0	2.1	0.1	12.2	0.0	26.4	155.1	195.8	184.1	211.7	395.8
Other hardwoods	8.0	0.4	2.6	11.0	0.1	0.0	0.5	0.0	1.1	6.7	8.4	10.1	9.3	19.4
Total	5,931.6	133.1	1,558.5	7,623.3	88.9	0.1	1,084.1	103.4	221.6	3,592.4	5,090.4	7,562.8	5,150.9	12,713.7
Unit total	6,489.3	547.4	1,673.3	8,710.0	126.9	5.2	1,206.1	105.5	221.6	4,117.5	5,782.8	8,702.1	5,790.7	14,492.8

(Table 10 continued on next page)

Table 10.—Continued

Prairie Unit

Softwoods													
Eastern redcedar	62.4	18.8	8.3	89.5	1.3	0.1	4.3	0.1	--	21.2	27.0	86.9	29.5	116.4
Shortleaf pine	0.9	0.0	0.1	1.0	0.0	--	0.0	--	--	0.4	0.5	1.0	0.5	1.5
White pine	0.6	0.0	0.1	0.7	0.0	--	0.0	--	--	0.4	0.4	0.6	0.4	1.1
Total	63.9	18.8	8.5	91.2	1.4	0.1	4.3	0.1	--	22.0	27.8	88.5	30.5	119.0
Hardwoods														
Ash	383.2	11.9	157.3	552.3	5.6	0.1	33.9	0.0	73.4	430.6	543.6	508.0	588.0	1,096.0
Basswood	10.2	0.2	4.2	14.7	0.1	--	0.9	--	2.0	11.6	14.6	13.5	15.8	29.3
River birch	27.0	0.8	10.5	38.2	0.3	--	2.2	--	4.8	28.3	35.6	35.1	38.7	73.8
Black cherry	14.3	0.3	5.3	19.9	0.2	0.0	1.1	0.0	2.4	14.4	18.1	18.3	19.8	38.1
Black walnut	1,022.0	4.1	152.4	1,178.6	0.6	0.2	1,050.3	0.1	385.1	543.6	1,979.9	2,462.5	696.0	3,158.4
Cottonwood	1,709.8	11.3	304.6	2,025.8	141.7	0.2	34.0	0.1	0.5	1,009.4	1,185.9	1,897.6	1,314.0	3,211.6
Elm	100.9	3.3	41.9	146.1	1.4	--	9.0	--	19.4	114.1	143.9	134.0	156.0	290.0
Hickory	509.1	13.5	210.4	733.0	6.9	0.0	45.2	0.0	98.1	575.5	725.8	672.9	785.9	1,458.8
Hard maple	12.9	0.2	4.1	17.2	0.1	0.0	0.8	0.0	1.8	10.5	13.2	15.8	14.6	30.4
Soft maple	744.4	29.8	304.3	1,078.5	12.3	0.8	66.3	0.3	142.1	834.4	1,056.2	996.0	1,138.7	2,134.7
Red oak group	4,056.4	112.1	1,032.8	5,201.3	69.4	0.0	607.8	97.1	0.0	2,575.4	3,349.7	4,942.8	3,608.2	8,551.0
White oak group	2,926.5	69.0	754.4	3,750.0	41.7	0.0	406.7	54.8	0.0	1,493.1	1,996.3	3,498.7	2,247.5	5,746.2
Sycamore	428.5	15.3	175.3	619.1	6.6	0.3	38.3	0.1	81.8	479.7	606.8	571.0	655.0	1,226.0
Other hardwoods	212.5	5.1	86.2	303.8	2.8	0.0	18.5	0.0	40.1	235.7	297.1	279.1	321.9	600.9
Total	12,157.8	277.0	3,243.7	15,678.5	289.7	1.7	2,315.0	152.5	851.6	8,356.4	11,966.8	16,045.2	11,600.0	27,645.2
Unit total	12,221.7	295.8	3,252.2	15,769.7	291.1	1.8	2,319.3	152.5	851.6	8,378.3	11,994.5	16,133.7	11,630.5	27,764.2

Table 10.—Continued

Riverborder Unit

	Source of material													
	Growing stock				Non-growing stock									
	Used for products		Logging residue (not used)	Total growing stock	Used for products					Logging slash (not used)	Total non-growing stock	Total wood material used	Total wood material not used	Total wood material harvested[a]
Species group	Saw-timber	Pole-timber			Limb-wood	Sap-lings	Cull trees	Dead trees	Non-forest trees					
Softwoods														
Eastern redcedar	489.2	220.6	77.1	787.0	18.1	1.5	58.7	0.8	--	263.7	342.8	788.9	340.8	1,129.7
Cypress	8.8	0.1	1.1	10.0	0.2	--	0.1	--	--	5.1	5.4	9.1	6.3	15.4
Shortleaf pine	90.7	11.9	11.0	113.6	1.5	0.2	0.8	0.0	--	47.0	49.6	105.1	58.0	163.1
White pine	1.0	0.0	0.1	1.2	0.0	--	0.0	--	--	0.6	0.6	1.0	0.7	1.8
Other pine	0.5	1.4	0.0	1.9	--	--	0.0	--	--	0.2	0.2	1.9	0.2	2.1
Total	590.2	234.0	89.4	913.6	19.8	1.7	59.6	0.8	--	316.6	398.5	906.1	406.1	1,312.2
Hardwoods														
Ash	141.9	6.8	56.8	205.5	4.4	0.2	14.0	0.1	25.4	150.3	194.6	192.9	207.1	400.0
River birch	2.9	4.6	0.7	8.2	0.9	0.3	0.3	0.1	0.3	2.5	4.4	9.4	3.2	12.7
Black cherry	48.0	1.2	17.7	66.9	1.8	0.0	4.9	0.0	8.1	48.0	62.9	64.1	65.7	129.8
Black walnut	250.0	2.2	37.2	289.4	0.4	0.1	255.5	0.0	93.5	127.6	477.2	601.9	164.8	766.7
Cottonwood	431.8	12.8	76.0	520.6	37.8	0.9	7.7	0.3	--	254.7	301.3	491.2	330.7	821.9
Elm	52.5	2.6	9.2	64.3	10.1	--	10.8	0.4	3.3	23.3	47.7	79.5	32.5	112.0
Hickory	332.5	9.1	134.4	475.9	7.7	0.0	31.7	0.1	60.2	355.0	454.8	441.3	489.4	930.7
Hard maple	109.3	2.5	42.2	154.1	2.6	0.0	10.1	0.0	19.5	115.0	147.3	144.2	157.2	301.4
Soft maple	147.3	6.6	60.2	214.1	2.8	0.2	13.2	0.1	28.1	165.4	209.8	198.4	225.6	424.0
Red oak group	2,960.4	81.7	748.3	3,790.5	56.7	0.0	445.6	70.5	0.0	1,865.2	2,437.9	3,614.8	2,613.5	6,228.4
White oak group	3,274.5	59.0	792.3	4,125.8	55.5	--	414.6	48.8	--	1,361.2	1,880.2	3,852.5	2,153.5	6,006.0
Sweetgum	52.6	2.0	14.5	69.1	6.1	--	8.2	0.2	6.2	38.6	59.3	75.3	53.1	128.4
Sycamore	194.0	14.2	78.5	286.7	4.6	0.7	17.3	0.2	36.6	216.0	275.5	267.7	294.4	562.2
Tupelo/gum	0.5	0.0	0.2	0.7	0.0	--	0.0	0.0	0.1	0.5	0.7	0.7	0.7	1.4
Yellow-poplar	239.9	5.4	98.9	344.2	3.3	--	21.3	0.0	46.2	271.0	341.8	316.1	369.9	686.0
Other hardwoods	240.3	14.1	24.0	278.5	59.7	0.0	58.2	2.2	5.1	54.0	179.2	379.5	78.1	457.6
Total	8,478.4	225.1	2,191.1	10,894.6	254.4	2.4	1,313.4	123.1	332.8	5,048.4	7,074.6	10,729.7	7,239.5	17,969.2
Unit total	9,068.6	459.1	2,280.5	11,808.2	274.2	4.0	1,373.1	124.0	332.8	5,365.0	7,473.1	11,635.8	7,645.6	19,281.3

All table cells without observations are indicated by --. Table value of 0.0 indicates the volume rounds to less than 0.1 thousand cubic feet. Columns and rows may not add to their totals due to rounding.

[a] Based on factors obtained from the Missouri Logging Utilization Study, 1987, and other regional utilization studies.

Table 11.—Growing-stock removals from timberland for industrial roundwood, in thousand cubic feet, by Forest Inventory Unit, county, and species group, Missouri, 2009

Forest Inventory Unit and county	All species	Softwoods						Hardwoods				
		Eastern redcedar	Cypress	Shortleaf pine	White pine	Other pine	Total softwoods	Ash	Basswood	River birch	Black cherry	Black walnut
Eastern Ozark Unit												
Bollinger	2,865	2	--	36	--	--	38	262	--	--	22	14
Butler	1,058	--	1	94	--	--	94	2	--	--	--	1
Carter	4,035	--	--	346	--	--	346	7	--	--	0	2
Crawford	2,146	5	--	54	--	--	60	5	--	0	0	12
Dent	2,230	17	--	76	--	--	93	2	--	--	--	21
Iron	2,659	42	--	59	--	--	101	2	--	--	0	1
Madison	5,147	29	--	286	--	--	315	35	--	--	9	6
Oregon	4,477	20	--	255	--	--	275	37	--	--	1	13
Reynolds	4,929	27	--	206	--	--	233	2	--	--	--	10
Ripley	3,752	71	--	349	--	--	420	11	--	0	1	2
Shannon	7,084	43	--	784	--	--	827	7	--	--	0	40
St. Francois	891	70	--	58	--	--	128	13	--	--	8	4
Washington	3,583	36	--	195	--	--	232	2	--	--	1	2
Wayne	2,433	8	1	175	--	--	184	14	--	--	1	3
Total	47,287	371	1	2,974	--	--	3,346	401	--	0	43	129
Southwestern Ozark Unit												
Barry	1,369	39	--	99	--	--	138	24	--	--	0	65
Christian	891	41	--	21	--	--	62	16	--	--	--	16
Douglas	2,473	54	--	128	--	--	182	1	--	--	--	35
Howell	4,830	20	--	424	--	--	443	9	--	--	5	29
McDonald	1,375	1	--	44	--	--	45	17	--	--	0	49
Newton	706	1	--	4	--	--	5	7	--	--	1	107
Ozark	1,146	156	--	154	--	--	310	0	--	--	1	2
Stone	660	10	--	10	--	--	20	23	--	--	0	71
Taney	853	358	--	33	--	--	391	1	--	--	0	10
Texas	5,183	7	--	452	--	--	459	5	--	--	0	78
Webster	415	30	--	--	--	--	30	0	--	--	--	37
Wright	870	7	--	9	--	--	16	1	--	--	--	43
Total	20,772	723	--	1,379	--	--	2,103	105	--	--	8	542

Table 11.—Continued

Forest Inventory Unit and county	All species	Softwoods						Hardwoods				
		Eastern redcedar	Cypress	Shortleaf pine	White pine	Other pine	Total softwoods	Ash	Basswood	River birch	Black cherry	Black walnut
Northwestern Ozark Unit												
Benton	168	12	--	--	--	--	12	3	--	0	0	29
Camden	863	182	--	--	--	--	182	8	--	--	0	20
Cedar	92	--	--	--	--	--	--	16	--	--	0	18
Dallas	726	131	--	--	--	--	131	18	--	--	0	22
Hickory	727	22	--	--	--	--	22	3	--	--	0	41
Laclede	316	74	--	2	--	--	76	0	--	--	0	18
Maries	883	147	--	--	--	--	147	14	--	--	0	11
Miller	1,428	290	--	--	--	--	290	12	--	--	0	27
Morgan	422	38	--	--	--	--	38	3	--	1	0	21
Phelps	2,042	70	--	24	--	--	94	8	--	--	--	28
Polk	478	21	--	--	--	--	21	100	--	--	--	48
Pulaski	374	70	--	4	--	--	74	1	--	--	--	30
St. Clair	190	0	--	--	--	--	0	4	--	0	0	44
Total	8,710	1,057	--	30	--	--	1,087	191	--	1	1	360
Prairie Unit												
Adair	352	--	--	--	--	--	--	2	7	--	1	79
Andrew	57	--	--	--	--	--	--	0	--	--	--	2
Atchison	13	--	--	--	--	--	--	--	--	--	--	7
Audrain	641	0	--	--	--	--	0	25	--	--	0	21
Barton	790	--	--	--	--	--	--	82	--	--	0	5
Bates	116	0	--	--	--	--	0	8	--	0	1	17
Buchanan	181	--	--	--	--	--	--	8	--	--	--	51
Caldwell	106	--	--	--	--	--	--	3	--	--	--	5
Carroll	380	--	--	--	--	--	--	14	--	--	--	0
Cass	299	0	--	--	--	--	0	4	--	0	0	2
Chariton	476	--	--	--	--	--	--	8	--	13	1	19
Clark	955	--	--	--	--	--	--	33	1	--	2	41
Clay	14	--	--	--	--	--	--	1	--	--	--	--
Clinton	21	--	--	--	--	--	--	0	--	--	--	6
Cooper	254	40	--	1	--	--	41	2	--	1	0	30

(Table 11 continued on next page)

Table 11.—Continued

Prairie Unit (cont.)

Dade	105	—	—	—	—	—	—	16	—	—	—	26
Daviess	552	—	—	—	—	—	—	28	—	—	0	22
De Kalb	51	—	—	—	—	—	—	1	—	—	—	6
Gentry	121	—	—	—	—	—	3	1	—	—	0	7
Greene	258	3	—	—	—	—	—	24	—	—	0	53
Grundy	381	—	—	—	—	—	—	21	—	—	—	22
Harrison	298	—	—	—	—	—	—	16	—	—	—	29
Henry	195	2	—	—	—	—	2	10	—	0	0	8
Holt	34	—	—	—	—	—	—	—	—	—	—	3
Jasper	148	—	—	—	—	—	—	12	—	—	0	21
Johnson	127	2	—	—	—	—	2	6	—	—	—	3
Knox	307	—	—	—	—	—	—	6	4	—	1	18
Lafayette	67	—	—	—	—	—	—	3	—	—	0	0
Lawrence	705	—	—	—	—	—	—	36	—	—	0	86
Lewis	570	0	—	—	0	—	1	18	2	—	1	42
Lincoln	628	0	—	1	—	—	1	21	—	—	1	8
Linn	117	—	—	—	—	—	—	2	—	—	0	13
Livingston	243	1	—	—	—	—	—	9	—	—	0	16
Macon	437	—	—	—	—	—	1	6	0	1	0	3
Marion	133	—	—	—	—	—	—	2	—	—	0	8
Mercer	204	—	—	—	—	—	—	13	—	—	0	17
Monroe	440	—	—	—	—	—	—	5	—	3	0	14
Nodaway	79	—	—	—	—	—	—	0	—	—	—	4
Pettis	352	41	—	—	—	—	41	5	—	2	0	67
Pike	686	0	—	—	—	—	0	39	—	—	0	7
Putnam	94	—	—	—	—	—	—	0	—	—	0	14
Ralls	582	—	—	—	—	—	—	24	—	—	0	8
Randolph	1,545	—	—	—	—	—	—	23	—	18	2	21
Ray	87	—	—	—	—	—	—	4	—	—	—	0
Saline	146	—	—	—	—	—	—	4	—	—	0	29
Schuyler	333	—	—	—	—	—	—	0	—	—	4	164
Scotland	516	—	—	—	—	—	—	6	—	—	4	72
Shelby	262	0	—	—	—	—	—	6	—	—	0	2
Sullivan	100	—	—	—	—	—	—	0	—	—	0	14
Vernon	178	0	—	—	—	—	0	6	—	0	0	65
Worth	39	—	—	—	—	—	—	0	—	0	—	3
Total	**15,770**	**89**	**—**	**1**	**1**	**—**	**91**	**552**	**15**	**38**	**20**	**1,179**

Table 11.—Continued

Forest Inventory Unit and county	All species	Softwoods						Hardwoods				
		Eastern redcedar	Cypress	Shortleaf pine	White pine	Other pine	Total softwoods	Ash	Basswood	River birch	Black cherry	Black walnut
Riverborder Unit												
Boone	541	0	--	--	--	--	0	7	--	6	1	40
Callaway	372	30	--	--	--	--	30	0	--	--	0	25
Cape Girardeau	854	9	--	12	--	--	21	23	--	--	10	11
Cole	531	101	--	1	--	--	102	11	--	--	0	9
Dunklin	78	--	0	2	--	--	2	5	--	--	--	0
Franklin	775	13	--	6	--	--	19	11	--	--	0	16
Gasconade	1,060	125	--	1	--	--	127	11	--	--	0	4
Howard	248	--	--	--	--	--	--	5	--	2	0	27
Jefferson	460	59	--	20	--	2	81	8	--	--	6	2
Mississippi	2	--	--	--	--	--	--	--	--	--	--	--
Moniteau	396	74	--	3	--	--	78	4	--	--	0	32
Montgomery	592	109	--	--	--	--	109	18	--	--	0	6
New Madrid	333	--	1	--	--	--	1	1	--	--	--	0
Osage	1,205	168	--	--	--	--	168	24	--	--	0	4
Pemiscot	1	--	--	--	--	--	--	--	--	--	--	--
Perry	2,562	20	--	22	--	--	42	58	--	--	36	81
Scott	82	--	0	--	--	--	0	1	--	--	0	0
St. Charles	141	1	--	1	0	--	2	2	--	--	2	5
St. Louis	32	1	--	--	--	--	1	0	--	--	0	2
Ste. Genevieve	711	63	--	42	--	--	105	14	--	--	9	10
Stoddard	448	--	9	3	--	--	12	0	--	--	1	5
Warren	386	15	--	0	1	--	16	3	--	--	2	9
Total	11,808	787	10	114	1	2	914	205	15	8	67	289
State total	104,347	3,028	11	4,497	2	2	7,540	1,455	15	48	139	2,499

(Table 11 continued on next page)

Table 11.—Continued

Forest Inventory Unit and county	Cotton-wood	Elm	Hickory	Hard maple	Soft maple	Red oak group	White oak group	Sweet-gum	Syca-more	Tupelo/gum	Yellow-poplar	Other hard-woods	Total hard-woods
Eastern Ozark Unit													
Bollinger	10	5	297	92	7	1,234	817	9	15	3	40	0	2,827
Butler	1	5	75	--	10	601	241	10	11	7	--	--	963
Carter	0	10	225	--	30	2,423	959	3	15	14	--	0	3,689
Crawford	7	6	81	8	7	1,175	755	2	27	1	--	2	2,086
Dent	6	1	133	1	6	1,214	734	0	19	--	--	1	2,137
Iron	4	0	100	4	7	1,633	792	0	11	4	--	0	2,559
Madison	8	8	383	62	7	2,511	1,691	15	44	27	26	0	4,832
Oregon	12	43	298	5	3	2,576	1,181	0	30	4	--	--	4,202
Reynolds	--	2	271	0	4	3,180	1,188	--	35	4	--	--	4,696
Ripley	5	15	202	1	15	2,169	853	21	26	7	--	4	3,331
Shannon	0	3	386	0	7	4,329	1,470	--	11	4	--	0	6,257
St. Francois	9	--	43	14	--	403	242	0	3	1	22	0	763
Washington	14	7	83	11	6	2,282	905	1	31	1	--	4	3,351
Wayne	0	6	200	15	8	1,256	710	6	19	11	--	0	2,248
Total	77	112	2,775	213	114	26,985	12,536	68	299	88	88	13	43,941
Southwestern Ozark Unit													
Barry	--	0	86	--	0	706	320	--	26	2	--	1	1,231
Christian	0	0	37	--	0	517	231	--	11	--	--	--	829
Douglas	0	2	57	--	7	1,636	545	--	7	--	--	--	2,291
Howell	1	4	259	1	5	2,764	1,284	--	13	10	--	5	4,387
McDonald	--	0	51	--	0	694	394	--	73	32	--	19	1,330
Newton	1	0	21	--	0	386	158	--	17	1	--	1	701
Ozark	0	0	18	--	0	602	188	--	23	--	--	--	836
Stone	--	0	26	--	0	348	159	--	13	--	--	0	640
Taney	2	1	12	--	1	294	132	--	8	--	--	0	462
Texas	--	0	196	0	5	3,226	1,206	--	8	0	--	0	4,724
Webster	--	0	18	--	0	213	116	--	0	--	--	--	385
Wright	--	0	26	--	4	574	206	--	1	--	--	--	855
Total	4	8	808	1	24	11,960	4,940	--	200	45	--	26	18,669

Table 11.—Continued

Forest Inventory Unit and county	Cotton-wood	Elm	Hickory	Hard maple	Soft maple	Red oak group	White oak group	Sweet-gum	Syca-more	Tupelo/gum	Yellow-poplar	Other hard-woods	Total hard-woods
Northwestern Ozark Unit													
Benton	0	--	3	--	1	62	54	--	2	--	--	2	156
Camden	1	0	19	3	2	288	329	1	10	--	--	1	681
Cedar	2	0	--	--	--	40	11	--	4	--	--	1	92
Dallas	--	7	46	--	0	239	248	--	14	--	--	--	595
Hickory	--	--	5	--	2	424	232	--	1	--	--	--	705
Laclede	--	0	7	--	2	116	95	--	0	--	--	--	239
Maries	24	6	18	3	26	168	428	--	36	--	--	1	736
Miller	14	0	23	19	15	464	532	9	23	--	--	1	1,139
Morgan	19	--	12	3	3	120	186	1	9	--	--	4	384
Phelps	6	9	85	1	4	853	878	0	74	--	--	1	1,948
Polk	1	--	9	--	0	160	124	--	14	--	--	--	457
Pulaski	--	4	15	--	2	112	127	--	10	--	--	--	300
St. Clair	2	0	15	--	1	83	36	--	3	--	--	1	190
Total	70	28	257	29	56	3,128	3,279	12	200	--	--	11	7,623
Prairie Unit													
Adair	8	2	8	1	22	85	136	--	0	--	--	1	352
Andrew	38	--	--	--	4	5	3	--	4	--	--	0	57
Atchison	4	--	--	0	0	--	1	--	--	--	--	--	13
Audrain	45	1	27	0	18	291	173	--	22	--	--	17	641
Barton	1	0	149	--	77	240	161	--	75	--	--	1	790
Bates	1	1	33	--	2	34	16	--	1	--	--	2	116
Buchanan	--	--	--	--	36	56	38	--	--	--	--	--	181
Caldwell	27	1	3	--	38	12	10	--	4	--	--	3	106
Carroll	181	5	11	--	47	61	26	--	17	--	--	18	380
Cass	0	0	26	--	1	105	97	--	25	--	--	38	299
Chariton	44	5	8	0	31	210	91	--	28	--	--	19	476
Clark	172	9	35	1	31	362	258	--	7	--	--	1	955
Clay	6	1	1	--	1	1	2	--	1	--	--	1	14
Clinton	3	0	0	--	2	4	3	--	1	--	--	0	21
Cooper	51	--	1	0	5	42	56	--	16	--	--	10	213

(Table 11 continued on next page)

Table 11.—Continued

Prairie Unit (cont.)

Dade	1	0	–	–	--	–	37	21	--	3	--	1	105
Daviess	206	22	28	0	--	65	48	68	--	43	--	21	552
De Kalb	26	1	1	–	--	3	5	4	--	4	--	1	51
Gentry	90	0	1	–	--	5	5	7	--	4	--	2	121
Greene	–	1	7	–	--	0	110	55	--	6	--	1	255
Grundy	136	15	21	–	--	48	39	38	--	26	--	15	381
Harrison	119	13	15	–	--	18	30	28	--	19	--	12	298
Henry	3	0	24	–	--	2	66	64	--	12	--	3	193
Holt	19	–	–	–	--	3	3	3	--	2	--	–	34
Jasper	1	0	5	–	--	3	69	32	--	4	--	2	148
Johnson	19	0	6	–	--	4	31	32	--	21	--	2	125
Knox	25	4	16	1	--	44	89	95	--	4	--	1	307
Lafayette	36	1	2	–	--	2	11	4	--	4	--	4	67
Lawrence	–	0	41	–	--	0	342	179	--	19	--	0	705
Lewis	52	8	21	2	--	42	155	218	--	8	--	1	569
Lincoln	91	0	23	3	--	35	228	182	--	24	--	11	627
Linn	6	1	4	0	--	31	35	24	--	1	--	0	117
Livingston	111	3	8	0	--	27	28	24	--	14	--	4	243
Macon	8	4	14	0	--	14	223	157	--	4	--	2	436
Marion	3	2	6	2	--	3	50	53	--	2	--	1	133
Mercer	58	12	13	0	--	15	24	26	--	13	--	14	204
Monroe	17	2	10	0	--	13	231	117	--	22	--	6	440
Nodaway	62	–	0	–	--	3	3	2	--	4	--	1	79
Pettis	21	–	4	1	--	5	81	83	--	28	--	15	311
Pike	101	0	39	3	--	43	316	85	--	30	--	22	686
Putnam	6	–	1	0	--	15	20	38	--	0	--	–	94
Ralls	23	1	26	1	--	26	238	212	--	8	--	15	582
Randolph	51	18	48	1	--	35	718	520	--	64	--	26	1,545
Ray	44	2	4	–	--	4	12	8	--	6	--	4	87
Saline	38	1	2	0	--	7	23	30	--	7	--	5	146
Schuyler	6	1	6	0	--	44	41	67	--	0	--	–	333
Scotland	31	3	12	0	--	168	142	74	--	3	--	0	516
Shelby	3	2	9	0	--	9	174	54	--	3	--	1	262
Sullivan	4	–	1	0	--	15	12	55	--	–	--	–	100
Vernon	3	0	14	–	--	13	51	21	--	3	--	2	178
Worth	28	–	0	–	--	2	3	3	--	0	--	0	39
Total	2,026	146	733	17	--	1,079	5,201	3,750	--	619	--	304	15,678

Table 11.—Continued

| | | | | | | Hardwoods | | | | | | | |
Forest Inventory Unit and county	Cotton-wood	Elm	Hickory	Hard maple	Soft maple	Red oak group	White oak group	Sweet-gum	Syca-more	Tupelo/gum	Yellow-poplar	Other hard-woods	Total hard-woods
Riverborder Unit													
Boone	25	4	19	1	11	192	200	--	34	--	--	4	541
Callaway	1	--	8	2	4	83	202	--	13	--	--	1	342
Cape Girardeau	10	0	81	24	--	342	292	1	0	0	37	1	833
Cole	18	1	10	5	19	163	172	1	19	--	--	1	430
Dunklin	0	1	6	--	1	34	19	6	2	--	--	--	75
Franklin	20	2	31	2	18	242	391	1	23	--	--	1	756
Gasconade	127	2	19	5	30	204	489	1	39	--	--	3	934
Howard	7	1	9	0	7	89	65	--	31	--	--	5	248
Jefferson	1	4	26	5	2	166	152	0	3	--	--	3	379
Mississippi	2	--	1	--	--	--	--	--	--	--	--	--	2
Moniteau	7	--	11	3	2	122	127	1	7	--	--	1	319
Montgomery	83	--	19	4	31	152	137	--	21	--	--	11	483
New Madrid	2	36	3	--	--	9	11	31	1	--	--	238	333
Osage	65	4	19	8	46	340	479	--	42	--	--	7	1,037
Pemiscot	--	0	--	--	1	--	--	--	--	--	--	--	1
Perry	11	1	124	70	1	1,139	738	2	3	1	256	0	2,520
Scott	2	0	11	4	--	5	19	14	1	--	25	--	82
St. Charles	46	0	1	3	14	24	31	--	10	--	--	0	139
St. Louis	--	--	1	0	1	3	23	--	0	--	--	0	31
Ste. Genevieve	8	--	36	15	2	267	218	1	1	--	26	1	606
Stoddard	7	7	40	0	2	168	175	11	19	--	--	1	436
Warren	77	0	2	4	23	47	184	--	18	--	--	0	370
Total	521	64	476	154	214	3,790	4,126	69	287	1	344	278	10,895
State total	2,697	358	5,048	414	1,487	51,065	28,631	149	1,604	134	432	632	96,807

All table cells without observations are indicated by --. Table value of 0 indicates the volume rounds to less than 1 thousand cubic feet. Columns and rows may not add to their totals due to rounding.

Table 12.—Sawtimber removals from timberland for industrial roundwood, in thousand board feet[a], by Forest Inventory Unit, county, and species group, Missouri, 2009

Forest Inventory Unit and county	All species	Softwoods						Hardwoods				
		Eastern redcedar	Cypress	Shortleaf pine	White pine	Other pine	Total softwoods	Ash	Basswood	River birch	Black cherry	Black walnut
Eastern Ozark Unit												
Bollinger	10,732	2	--	175	--	--	177	1,009	--	--	83	64
Butler	3,955	--	3	400	--	--	403	6	--	--	--	6
Carter	15,097	--	--	1,526	--	--	1,526	29	--	--	0	8
Crawford	8,304	6	--	261	--	--	267	19	--	1	0	53
Dent	8,586	19	--	302	--	--	321	9	--	--	--	93
Iron	10,043	58	--	242	--	--	299	7	--	--	0	4
Madison	19,387	43	--	1,456	--	--	1,499	134	--	--	35	26
Oregon	16,598	25	--	1,069	--	--	1,094	142	--	--	2	57
Reynolds	18,602	30	--	981	--	--	1,010	8	--	--	--	45
Ripley	13,914	79	--	1,535	--	--	1,613	41	--	0	3	7
Shannon	26,186	60	--	3,001	--	--	3,061	25	--	--	1	179
St. Francois	3,427	186	--	303	--	--	490	50	--	--	32	19
Washington	13,742	73	--	828	--	--	901	9	--	--	6	10
Wayne	9,115	9	3	794	--	--	806	54	--	--	3	13
Total	177,689	590	6	12,874	--	--	13,469	1,544	--	1	166	582
Southwestern Ozark Unit												
Barry	5,175	52	--	507	--	--	560	93	--	--	1	294
Christian	3,214	45	--	109	--	--	154	61	--	--	--	72
Douglas	9,133	60	--	648	--	--	708	5	--	--	--	158
Howell	18,426	25	--	1,857	--	--	1,882	34	--	--	21	131
McDonald	5,570	6	--	234	--	--	239	67	--	--	1	220
Newton	2,720	6	--	23	--	--	28	28	--	--	3	484
Ozark	4,025	172	--	784	--	--	955	2	--	--	5	10
Stone	2,476	11	--	51	--	--	62	88	--	--	0	317
Taney	2,270	394	--	170	--	--	563	4	--	--	1	44
Texas	19,054	10	--	1,550	--	--	1,560	19	--	--	0	353
Webster	1,475	33	--	--	--	--	33	1	--	--	--	164
Wright	3,224	7	--	48	--	--	55	3	--	--	--	192
Total	76,761	820	--	5,980	--	--	6,800	407	--	--	32	2,439

Table 12.—Continued

Forest Inventory Unit and county	All species	Softwoods						Hardwoods				
		Eastern redcedar	Cypress	Shortleaf pine	White pine	Other pine	Total softwoods	Ash	Basswood	River birch	Black cherry	Black walnut
Northwestern Ozark Unit												
Benton	664	54	--	--	--	--	54	11	--	2	--	131
Camden	2,830	201	--	--	--	--	201	31	--	--	0	91
Cedar	361	--	--	--	--	--	--	62	--	--	0	81
Dallas	2,357	145	--	--	--	--	145	71	--	--	1	100
Hickory	2,640	24	--	--	--	--	24	10	--	--	0	185
Laclede	990	82	--	12	--	--	94	0	--	--	0	82
Maries	3,800	645	--	--	--	--	645	56	--	--	0	51
Miller	5,407	1,066	--	--	--	--	1,066	47	--	--	0	124
Morgan	1,745	161	--	--	--	--	161	12	--	5	0	94
Phelps	7,991	268	--	100	--	--	368	29	--	--	--	127
Polk	1,763	23	--	--	--	--	23	385	--	--	--	218
Pulaski	1,494	268	--	13	--	--	281	6	--	--	--	137
St. Clair	743	0	--	--	--	--	0	16	--	0	1	198
Total	32,786	2,938	--	125	--	--	3,062	737	--	8	3	1,620
Prairie Unit												
Adair	1,427	--	--	--	--	--	--	9	26	--	3	357
Andrew	289	--	--	--	--	--	--	0	--	--	--	8
Atchison	61	--	--	--	--	--	--	--	--	--	--	30
Audrain	2,596	0	--	--	--	--	0	95	--	--	0	94
Barton	2,971	--	--	--	--	--	--	315	--	--	0	23
Bates	449	0	--	--	--	--	0	33	--	1	3	75
Buchanan	711	--	--	--	--	--	--	--	--	--	--	228
Caldwell	456	--	--	--	--	--	--	12	--	--	--	20
Carroll	1,795	--	--	--	--	--	--	52	--	--	--	0
Cass	1,115	0	--	--	--	--	0	14	--	0	1	7
Chariton	1,864	--	--	--	--	--	--	28	--	50	4	84
Clark	3,892	--	--	--	--	--	--	125	6	--	7	184
Clay	63	--	--	--	--	--	--	3	--	--	--	--
Clinton	87	--	--	--	--	--	--	1	--	--	--	28
Cooper	1,089	163	--	4	--	--	167	6	--	5	0	132

(Table 12 continued on next page)

Table 12.—Continued

Prairie Unit (cont.)

Dade	415	--	--	--	--	62	--	--	119
Daviess	2,518	--	--	--	--	109	--	0	97
De Kalb	245	--	--	--	--	2	--	--	29
Gentry	641	--	--	--	--	4	--	--	31
Greene	989	3	--	--	3	91	--	0	239
Grundy	1,730	--	--	--	--	80	--	--	97
Harrison	1,382	--	--	--	--	60	--	--	131
Henry	732	2	--	--	2	38	--	0	1	37
Holt	168	--	--	--	--	--	--	--	15
Jasper	565	--	--	--	--	46	--	0	92
Johnson	508	2	--	--	2	22	--	--	12
Knox	1,212	--	--	--	--	22	17	3	78
Lafayette	324	--	--	--	--	10	--	0	0
Lawrence	2,670	--	--	--	--	139	--	0	388
Lewis	2,265	0	--	2	2	67	7	4	187
Lincoln	2,675	0	--	4	4	81	--	3	37
Linn	467	--	--	--	--	7	--	0	57
Livingston	1,156	--	--	--	--	33	--	0	72
Macon	1,747	1	--	--	1	25	1	3	2	13
Marion	525	--	--	--	--	9	--	1	38
Mercer	904	--	--	--	--	49	--	0	76
Monroe	1,711	--	--	--	--	18	--	13	1	62
Nodaway	423	--	--	--	--	0	--	--	18
Pettis	1,471	209	--	--	209	22	--	8	1	298
Pike	2,803	0	--	--	0	149	--	0	33
Putnam	387	--	--	--	--	1	--	0	62
Ralls	2,429	--	--	--	--	92	--	2	38
Randolph	5,934	--	--	--	--	88	--	70	7	95
Ray	414	--	--	--	--	16	--	--	0
Saline	616	--	--	--	--	12	--	0	124
Schuyler	1,394	--	--	--	--	2	--	14	737
Scotland	2,048	--	--	--	--	21	--	17	322
Shelby	995	0	--	--	0	23	--	0	9
Sullivan	432	--	--	--	--	1	--	0	62
Vernon	718	0	--	--	0	24	--	0	292
Worth	203	--	--	--	--	1	--	--	15
Total	64,681	382	5	4	391	2,119	57	151	77	5,284

Table 12.—Continued

Forest Inventory Unit and county	All species	Softwoods						Hardwoods				
		Eastern redcedar	Cypress	Shortleaf pine	White pine	Other pine	Total softwoods	Ash	Basswood	River birch	Black cherry	Black walnut
Riverborder Unit												
Boone	2,045	0	--	--	--	--	0	23	--	6	2	173
Callaway	1,554	88	--	--	--	--	88	1	--	--	1	113
Cape Girardeau	3,249	10	--	61	--	--	71	90	--	--	39	50
Cole	2,142	491	--	4	--	--	495	39	--	--	0	39
Dunklin	293	--	2	10	--	--	12	21	--	--	--	1
Franklin	3,195	14	--	30	--	--	44	41	--	--	0	70
Gasconade	4,721	557	--	8	--	--	564	41	--	--	0	19
Howard	943	557	--	--	--	--	--	14	--	9	1	119
Jefferson	1,654	87	--	62	--	3	151	34	--	--	24	8
Mississippi	13	--	--	--	--	--	--	--	--	--	--	--
Moniteau	1,392	177	--	17	--	--	194	16	--	--	0	141
Montgomery	2,676	557	--	--	--	--	557	71	--	--	1	29
New Madrid	1,398	--	3	--	--	--	3	5	--	--	--	1
Osage	4,739	717	--	--	--	--	717	91	--	--	0	18
Pemiscot	4	--	--	--	--	--	--	--	--	--	--	--
Perry	9,722	22	--	112	--	--	134	222	--	--	138	366
Scott	318	--	1	--	--	--	1	3	--	--	0	2
St. Charles	638	1	--	3	2	--	7	6	--	--	8	24
St. Louis	142	1	--	--	--	--	1	1	--	--	0	9
Ste. Genevieve	2,676	102	--	210	--	--	312	55	--	--	35	47
Stoddard	1,693	--	45	15	--	--	60	1	--	--	3	23
Warren	1,793	71	--	2	4	--	77	11	--	--	6	41
Total	47,000	2,895	51	532	6	3	3,488	785	57	15	260	1,293
State total	398,917	7,625	57	19,516	9	3	27,210	5,592	57	175	539	11,218

(Table 12 continued on next page)

Table 12.—Continued

Forest Inventory Unit and county	Cotton-wood	Elm	Hickory	Hard maple	Soft maple	Red oak group	White oak group	Sweet-gum	Syca-more	Tupelo/gum	Yellow-poplar	Other hard-woods	Total hard-woods
Eastern Ozark Unit													
Bollinger	60	18	1,134	354	27	4,501	3,046	35	58	11	154	0	10,555
Butler	3	21	288	--	37	2,198	884	40	41	28	--	0	3,552
Carter	1	40	866	--	114	8,864	3,523	11	58	56	--	0	13,571
Crawford	38	25	314	30	26	4,304	3,105	6	105	2	--	7	8,037
Dent	33	5	511	3	21	4,436	3,075	0	75	--	--	4	8,266
Iron	22	1	384	16	29	5,978	3,243	0	41	16	--	2	9,743
Madison	45	29	1,475	239	28	9,188	6,255	57	171	104	100	1	17,888
Oregon	71	165	1,148	20	10	9,423	4,337	1	115	14	--	0	15,504
Reynolds	--	8	1,043	1	15	11,630	4,690	--	136	16	--	0	17,592
Ripley	31	58	780	5	56	7,941	3,152	80	102	28	--	16	12,301
Shannon	2	12	1,485	1	26	15,821	5,513	--	43	16	--	1	23,125
St. Francois	52	--	164	54	--	1,476	988	1	12	3	86	1	2,938
Washington	83	29	333	44	22	8,409	3,748	4	121	5	--	18	12,841
Wayne	2	23	770	57	31	4,594	2,621	24	73	43	--	0	8,309
Total	443	434	10,696	825	441	98,763	48,180	260	1,153	342	340	51	164,220
Southwestern Ozark Unit													
Barry	--	1	330	--	1	2,597	1,177	--	110	8	--	3	4,615
Christian	2	0	144	--	1	1,891	847	--	42	--	--	0	3,060
Douglas	2	6	220	--	29	5,985	1,995	--	26	--	--	0	8,425
Howell	3	15	995	2	18	10,328	4,882	--	50	43	--	21	16,544
McDonald	--	1	196	--	--	2,791	1,534	--	324	122	--	73	5,331
Newton	4	1	82	--	2	1,426	584	--	70	5	--	3	2,691
Ozark	2	0	69	--	1	2,204	688	--	89	--	--	0	3,070
Stone	--	1	102	--	1	1,275	580	--	48	--	--	0	2,413
Taney	11	5	48	--	3	1,074	483	--	32	--	--	2	1,707
Texas	--	0	738	0	18	11,795	4,538	--	32	0	--	0	17,494
Webster	--	0	70	--	2	781	423	--	0	--	--	0	1,442
Wright	--	0	98	--	17	2,102	752	--	4	--	--	0	3,169
Total	22	31	3,093	2	94	44,249	18,484	--	828	178	--	103	69,961

Table 12.—Continued

Forest Inventory Unit and county	Cotton-wood	Elm	Hickory	Hard maple	Soft maple	Red oak group	White oak group	Sweet-gum	Syca-more	Tupelo/gum	Yellow-poplar	Other hard-woods	Total hard-woods
Northwestern Ozark Unit													
Benton	2	--	13	--	5	226	204	--	8	--	--	7	610
Camden	7	0	72	11	7	1,053	1,313	6	37	--	--	0	2,629
Cedar	11	1	--	--	--	146	40	--	16	--	--	3	361
Dallas	--	28	177	--	1	874	906	--	55	--	--	0	2,213
Hickory	--	0	18	--	--	1,550	848	--	4	--	--	0	2,616
Laclede	--	0	29	--	6	423	353	--	2	--	--	0	897
Maries	142	23	69	12	100	613	1,946	--	138	--	--	5	3,155
Miller	78	2	88	72	57	1,698	2,049	34	88	--	--	3	4,341
Morgan	109	--	48	11	15	439	791	6	34	--	--	20	1,584
Phelps	34	36	327	5	15	3,122	3,634	1	286	--	--	4	7,622
Polk	8	--	33	--	1	587	452	--	55	--	--	0	1,740
Pulaski	--	14	56	--	6	410	547	--	37	--	--	0	1,213
St. Clair	12	2	58	--	4	304	133	--	10	--	--	4	743
Total	403	106	989	112	218	11,446	13,217	47	770	--	--	46	29,724
Prairie Unit													
Adair	44	7	32	4	84	311	545	--	2	--	--	5	1,427
Andrew	220	--	--	--	16	18	11	--	16	--	--	1	289
Atchison	25	3	--	0	0	--	5	--	--	--	--	0	61
Audrain	262	3	105	0	68	1,066	749	--	86	--	--	67	2,595
Barton	4	1	574	--	298	879	588	--	287	--	--	2	2,971
Bates	6	4	126	--	6	126	59	--	5	--	--	6	449
Buchanan	--	--	--	--	139	206	138	--	--	--	--	0	711
Caldwell	153	6	11	--	147	45	35	--	14	--	--	11	456
Carroll	1,046	19	41	--	183	223	95	--	67	--	--	68	1,795
Cass	3	2	102	--	3	385	356	--	97	--	--	146	1,115
Chariton	253	20	33	0	92	767	352	--	109	--	--	73	1,864
Clark	979	35	132	4	117	1,323	951	--	27	--	--	4	3,892
Clay	32	3	3	--	3	3	8	--	6	--	--	3	63
Clinton	16	1	1	--	9	14	12	--	3	--	--	1	87
Cooper	296	--	4	0	13	155	213	--	56	--	--	41	922

(Table 12 continued on next page)

75

Table 12.—Continued

Prairie Unit (cont.)

Dade	8	1	—	—	—	136	76	—	11	—	2	415
Daviess	1,188	86	109	0	252	176	251	—	167	—	82	2,518
De Kalb	146	2	2	—	13	18	15	—	15	—	3	245
Gentry	517	2	3	—	18	17	25	—	16	—	8	641
Greene	—	2	25	—	1	403	201	—	21	—	2	986
Grundy	787	58	80	—	185	144	139	—	101	—	57	1,730
Harrison	686	49	59	—	70	109	101	—	73	—	46	1,382
Henry	18	2	91	—	7	243	235	—	47	—	11	729
Holt	112	—	—	—	10	13	10	—	9	—	0	168
Jasper	4	2	20	—	10	253	115	—	15	—	7	565
Johnson	109	1	24	—	15	114	118	—	83	—	9	506
Knox	132	15	58	4	167	325	372	—	14	—	5	1,212
Lafayette	209	4	8	—	9	41	16	—	14	—	14	324
Lawrence	—	2	158	—	1	1,252	654	—	74	—	1	2,670
Lewis	285	30	79	7	161	565	837	—	30	—	4	2,263
Lincoln	524	2	88	13	134	833	821	—	94	—	43	2,672
Linn	36	2	14	0	120	127	97	—	5	—	1	467
Livingston	641	13	32	0	104	101	94	—	53	—	14	1,156
Macon	48	15	52	0	53	814	695	—	16	—	9	1,746
Marion	15	7	23	7	11	185	216	—	10	—	4	525
Mercer	334	48	49	0	56	88	100	—	51	—	52	904
Monroe	96	9	39	0	50	846	471	—	83	—	23	1,711
Nodaway	355	—	1	—	13	12	7	—	14	—	2	423
Pettis	119	—	17	3	22	298	303	—	109	—	62	1,262
Pike	583	2	151	13	165	1,157	349	—	114	—	86	2,803
Putnam	33	—	2	0	58	74	157	—	0	—	0	387
Ralls	135	2	99	4	100	871	997	—	32	—	57	2,429
Randolph	293	71	187	4	135	2,627	2,009	—	248	—	100	5,934
Ray	252	7	14	—	15	43	28	—	23	—	16	414
Saline	199	4	7	0	17	83	129	—	20	—	19	616
Schuyler	33	3	24	0	171	149	260	—	2	—	0	1,394
Scotland	166	12	44	2	645	520	286	—	12	—	2	2,048
Shelby	19	7	33	2	35	635	220	—	10	—	2	995
Sullivan	23	—	2	0	59	43	243	—	—	—	0	432
Vernon	15	2	55	—	51	185	75	—	10	—	7	718
Worth	161	—	1	—	6	6	12	—	1	—	0	203
Total	11,625	558	2,814	67	4,114	19,026	14,849	—	2,371	—	1,178	64,290

Table 12.—Continued

Forest Inventory Unit and county	Cotton-wood	Elm	Hickory	Hard maple	Soft maple	Red oak group	White oak group	Sweet-gum	Syca-more	Tupelo/ gum	Yellow-poplar	Other hard-woods	Total hard-woods
Riverborder Unit													
Boone	98	14	74	4	30	701	786	--	120	--	--	14	2,045
Callaway	8	--	32	6	16	306	926	--	52	--	--	4	1,466
Cape Girardeau	58	1	313	93	--	1,250	1,134	2	2	0	143	4	3,178
Cole	104	6	37	20	74	596	650	6	72	--	--	5	1,647
Dunklin	2	3	22	--	5	125	71	22	9	--	--	0	280
Franklin	116	8	118	7	70	885	1,745	3	87	--	--	3	3,152
Gasconade	735	9	72	19	116	746	2,235	3	149	--	--	11	4,157
Howard	35	5	36	0	28	324	258	--	95	--	--	20	943
Jefferson	7	17	104	22	9	623	630	1	12	--	--	12	1,503
Mississippi	11	--	2	--	--	--	--	--	--	--	--	0	13
Moniteau	12	--	42	11	9	448	480	6	28	--	--	5	1,198
Montgomery	481	--	74	16	118	557	649	--	79	--	--	43	2,119
New Madrid	13	152	10	--	177	35	40	129	5	--	--	1,005	1,395
Osage	374	15	72	29	177	1,244	1,811	--	162	--	--	27	4,022
Pemiscot	--	2	--	--	2	--	--	--	--	--	--	0	4
Perry	66	3	479	270	3	4,167	2,866	7	10	3	987	2	9,588
Scott	12	1	41	15	--	17	74	52	3	--	97	0	316
St. Charles	266	1	5	12	54	89	128	--	39	--	--	0	632
St. Louis	--	--	4	0	4	12	110	--	0	--	--	0	141
Ste. Genevieve	45	--	140	56	--	975	899	4	4	--	100	4	2,364
Stoddard	42	27	153	0	9	614	643	41	74	--	--	4	1,634
Warren	445	0	9	16	90	172	856	--	70	--	--	0	1,716
Total	2,930	263	1,840	597	813	13,886	16,992	275	1,071	3	1,326	1,164	43,512
State total	15,423	1,392	19,432	1,603	5,680	187,371	111,722	582	6,193	522	1,667	2,542	371,707

All table cells without observations are indicated by --. Table value of 0 indicates the volume rounds to less than 1 thousand board feet. Columns and rows may not add to their totals due to rounding.

[a] International ¼-inch rule.

Table 13.—Harvest residue generated by industrial roundwood harvesting, in thousand cubic feet, by Forest Inventory Unit, county, and species group, Missouri, 2009

Forest Inventory Unit and county	All species	Softwoods						Hardwoods				
		Eastern redcedar	Cypress	Shortleaf pine	White pine	Other pine	Total softwoods	Ash	Basswood	River birch	Black cherry	Black walnut
Eastern Ozark Unit												
Bollinger	2,135	2	--	21	--	--	23	175	--	--	23	8
Butler	760	--	0	49	--	--	49	2	--	--	--	1
Carter	2,841	--	--	182	--	--	182	8	--	--	0	1
Crawford	1,406	5	--	31	--	--	36	5	--	0	0	7
Dent	1,462	15	--	37	--	--	52	3	--	--	--	12
Iron	1,766	35	--	27	--	--	63	2	--	--	0	0
Madison	3,757	24	--	176	--	--	200	37	--	--	10	3
Oregon	3,194	13	--	124	--	--	137	39	--	--	1	7
Reynolds	3,400	24	--	118	--	--	142	2	--	--	--	6
Ripley	2,634	63	--	184	--	--	247	10	--	0	0	1
Shannon	4,769	19	--	339	--	--	358	7	--	--	0	23
St. Francois	603	42	--	24	--	--	66	14	--	--	9	2
Washington	2,191	27	--	93	--	--	119	2	--	--	0	1
Wayne	1,743	7	0	96	--	--	103	15	--	--	1	1
Total	32,660	277	1	1,501	--	--	1,778	319	--	0	44	74
Southwestern Ozark Unit												
Barry	979	33	--	58	--	--	91	26	--	--	0	39
Christian	648	36	--	13	--	--	49	17	--	--	--	10
Douglas	1,741	48	--	79	--	--	127	1	--	--	--	21
Howell	2,771	13	--	218	--	--	231	6	--	--	1	17
McDonald	859	0	--	14	--	--	14	19	--	--	0	29
Newton	486	0	--	1	--	--	1	8	--	--	1	65
Ozark	828	138	--	95	--	--	233	0	--	--	1	1
Stone	477	9	--	6	--	--	15	25	--	--	0	43
Taney	664	315	--	6	--	--	336	1	--	--	0	6
Texas	3,468	3	--	181	--	--	184	5	--	--	0	46
Webster	296	26	--	--	--	--	26	0	--	--	--	22
Wright	613	6	--	6	--	--	12	1	--	--	--	25
Total	13,828	627	--	692	--	--	1,319	109	--	--	4	324

Table 13.—Continued

Forest Inventory Unit and county	All species	Softwoods						Hardwoods				
		Eastern redcedar	Cypress	Shortleaf pine	White pine	Other pine	Total soft-woods	Ash	Bass-wood	River birch	Black cherry	Black walnut
Northwestern Ozark Unit												
Benton	108	3	--	--	--	--	3	2	--	0	--	17
Camden	607	161	--	--	--	--	161	9	--	--	0	12
Cedar	71	--	--	--	--	--	--	17	--	--	0	11
Dallas	560	116	--	--	--	--	116	20	--	--	0	13
Hickory	508	19	--	--	--	--	19	3	--	--	0	25
Laclede	233	66	--	1	--	--	67	0	--	--	0	11
Maries	479	46	--	--	--	--	46	15	--	--	0	7
Miller	919	125	--	--	--	--	125	13	--	--	0	16
Morgan	240	13	--	--	--	--	13	2	--	0	0	12
Phelps	1,331	28	--	12	--	--	40	8	--	--	--	17
Polk	378	19	--	--	--	--	19	107	--	--	--	29
Pulaski	220	28	--	2	--	--	30	1	--	--	--	18
St. Clair	137	0	--	--	--	--	0	5	--	0	0	26
Total	5,791	625	--	15	--	--	640	203	--	0	1	213
Prairie Unit												
Adair	239	--	--	--	--	--	--	2	7	--	1	48
Andrew	40	--	--	--	--	--	--	0	--	--	--	1
Atchison	8	--	--	--	--	--	--	--	--	--	--	4
Audrain	448	0	--	--	--	--	0	27	--	--	0	13
Barton	694	--	--	--	--	--	0	88	--	--	0	3
Bates	97	0	--	--	--	--	0	9	--	0	1	10
Buchanan	132	--	--	--	--	--	--	--	--	--	--	28
Caldwell	91	--	--	--	--	--	--	3	--	--	--	2
Carroll	299	--	--	--	--	--	--	15	--	--	--	0
Cass	244	0	--	--	--	--	0	4	--	0	0	1
Chariton	355	--	--	--	--	--	--	8	--	14	1	11
Clark	689	--	--	--	--	--	--	35	2	--	2	25
Clay	11	--	--	--	--	--	--	1	--	--	--	--
Clinton	14	--	--	--	--	--	--	0	--	--	--	3
Cooper	156	14	--	0	--	--	15	0	--	--	0	18

(Table 13 continued on next page)

Table 13.—Continued

Prairie Unit (cont.)

Dade	78	--	--	--	--	--	--	17	--	--	--	16
Daviess	450	--	--	--	--	--	--	31	--	--	0	12
De Kalb	36	--	--	--	--	--	--	1	--	--	--	3
Gentry	85	--	--	--	--	--	--	1	--	--	--	4
Greene	188	3	--	--	--	3	--	25	--	--	0	31
Grundy	312	--	--	--	--	--	--	22	--	--	--	12
Harrison	233	--	--	--	--	--	--	17	--	--	--	17
Henry	154	2	--	--	--	2	--	11	--	0	0	5
Holt	24	--	--	--	--	--	--	--	--	--	--	2
Jasper	111	--	--	--	--	--	--	13	--	--	0	12
Johnson	102	2	--	--	--	2	--	6	--	--	--	2
Knox	229	--	--	--	--	--	--	6	5	--	1	10
Lafayette	50	--	--	--	--	--	--	3	--	--	0	0
Lawrence	519	--	--	--	--	--	--	39	--	--	0	52
Lewis	409	0	--	0	--	1	--	19	2	--	1	25
Lincoln	428	0	--	0	0	0	--	23	--	--	1	5
Linn	92	--	--	--	--	--	--	2	--	--	0	8
Livingston	185	--	--	--	--	--	--	9	--	--	0	9
Macon	284	1	--	--	--	1	--	7	0	1	1	2
Marion	90	--	--	--	--	--	--	3	--	--	0	5
Mercer	167	--	--	--	--	--	--	14	--	--	0	10
Monroe	314	--	--	--	--	--	--	5	--	4	0	8
Nodaway	54	--	--	--	--	--	--	0	--	--	--	2
Pettis	224	7	--	--	--	7	--	4	--	0	0	40
Pike	526	0	--	--	--	0	--	42	--	--	0	4
Putnam	64	--	--	--	--	--	--	0	--	--	0	8
Ralls	371	--	--	--	--	--	--	26	--	--	0	5
Randolph	1,124	--	--	--	--	--	--	25	--	20	2	13
Ray	67	--	--	--	--	--	--	4	--	--	--	0
Saline	92	--	--	--	--	--	--	3	--	--	0	17
Schuyler	233	--	--	--	--	--	--	6	--	--	4	100
Scotland	416	--	--	--	--	--	--	6	--	--	5	43
Shelby	186	0	--	--	--	0	--	7	--	--	0	1
Sullivan	62	--	--	--	--	--	--	0	--	--	0	8
Vernon	131	0	--	--	--	0	--	7	--	0	0	38
Worth	26	--	--	--	--	--	--	0	--	--	--	1
Total	11,630	29	--	1	0	30	--	588	16	39	20	696

Table 13.—Continued

Forest Inventory Unit and county	All species	Softwoods						Hardwoods				
		Eastern redcedar	Cypress	Shortleaf pine	White pine	Other pine	Total softwoods	Ash	Basswood	River birch	Black cherry	Black walnut
Riverborder Unit												
Boone	365	0	--	--	--	--	0	6	--	1	0	23
Callaway	195	17	--	--	--	--	17	0	--	--	0	15
Cape Girardeau	607	8	--	7	--	--	15	24	--	--	11	5
Cole	338	23	--	0	--	--	23	11	--	--	0	5
Dunklin	62	--	0	1	--	--	1	6	--	--	--	0
Franklin	459	11	--	4	--	--	15	11	--	--	0	9
Gasconade	587	37	--	1	--	--	38	11	--	--	0	2
Howard	176	--	--	--	--	--	--	4	--	2	0	16
Jefferson	240	48	--	7	--	0	55	2	--	--	2	1
Mississippi	2	--	--	--	--	--	--	--	--	--	--	--
Moniteau	271	49	--	2	--	--	51	4	--	--	0	19
Montgomery	343	19	--	--	--	--	19	20	--	--	0	4
New Madrid	76	--	0	--	--	--	0	0	--	--	--	0
Osage	799	55	--	--	--	--	55	25	--	--	0	2
Pemiscot	0	--	--	--	--	--	--	--	--	--	--	--
Perry	1,897	18	--	14	--	--	31	62	--	--	39	45
Scott	73	--	0	--	--	--	0	0	--	--	0	0
St. Charles	101	1	--	0	0	--	1	2	--	--	2	3
St. Louis	14	1	--	--	--	--	1	0	--	--	0	1
Ste. Genevieve	495	50	--	20	--	--	70	15	--	--	10	6
Stoddard	336	--	5	2	--	--	7	0	--	--	1	3
Warren	209	4	--	0	0	0	4	3	--	--	1	5
Total	7,646	341	6	58	1	0	406	207	--	3	66	165
State total	71,555	1,899	7	2,267	1	0	4,174	1,427	16	42	135	1,472

(Table 13 continued on next page)

Table 13.—Continued

Forest Inventory Unit and county	Cotton-wood	Elm	Hickory	Hard maple	Soft maple	Red oak group	White oak group	Sweet-gum	Syca-more	Tupelo/gum	Yellow-poplar	Other hard-woods	Total hard-woods
Eastern Ozark Unit													
Bollinger	7	5	316	99	8	855	544	10	16	3	43	0	2,112
Butler	0	6	80	--	10	417	166	11	11	8	--	--	712
Carter	0	11	240	--	32	1,680	652	3	16	16	--	0	2,659
Crawford	4	6	83	8	7	809	409	2	29	0	--	2	1,370
Dent	4	1	142	1	6	841	377	0	21	--	--	1	1,410
Iron	2	0	105	4	8	1,132	433	0	12	4	--	0	1,703
Madison	5	8	411	67	8	1,743	1,145	16	48	29	28	0	3,557
Oregon	8	46	319	6	3	1,787	804	0	32	4	--	--	3,056
Reynolds	--	2	290	0	4	2,206	706	--	38	4	--	--	3,258
Ripley	4	16	211	1	15	1,501	569	22	27	7	--	3	2,387
Shannon	0	3	409	0	7	2,991	954	--	12	4	--	0	4,411
St. Francois	6	--	46	15	--	280	136	0	3	1	24	0	537
Washington	9	2	59	4	5	1,527	430	1	29	0	--	2	2,072
Wayne	0	6	213	16	9	871	467	7	20	12	--	0	1,640
Total	50	113	2,924	220	121	18,641	7,792	72	314	92	95	9	30,882
Southwestern Ozark Unit													
Barry	--	0	92	--	0	485	221	--	21	1	--	1	888
Christian	0	0	40	--	0	359	161	--	12	--	--	--	599
Douglas	0	2	61	--	8	1,135	378	--	7	--	--	--	1,614
Howell	0	2	191	1	5	1,640	662	--	12	2	--	1	2,540
McDonald	--	0	55	--	0	398	236	--	53	34	--	20	844
Newton	0	0	23	--	1	263	108	--	14	1	--	1	485
Ozark	0	0	19	--	0	418	131	--	25	--	--	--	595
Stone	--	0	28	--	0	242	110	--	13	--	--	0	461
Taney	1	1	13	--	1	204	92	--	9	--	--	0	328
Texas	--	0	203	0	5	2,236	780	--	9	0	--	0	3,284
Webster	--	0	19	--	0	148	80	--	0	--	--	--	270
Wright	--	0	27	--	5	399	143	--	1	--	--	--	601
Total	2	7	771	1	26	7,927	3,102	--	176	37	--	24	12,509

Table 13.—Continued

Forest Inventory Unit and county	Cotton-wood	Elm	Hickory	Hard maple	Soft maple	Red oak group	White oak group	Sweet-gum	Syca-more	Tupelo/gum	Yellow-poplar	Other hard-woods	Total hard-woods
Northwestern Ozark Unit													
Benton	0	--	4	--	1	43	35	--	1	--	--	1	105
Camden	1	0	20	3	2	200	188	2	10	--	--	--	446
Cedar	1	0	--	--	--	28	8	--	5	--	--	1	71
Dallas	--	8	49	--	0	166	172	--	15	--	--	--	444
Hickory	--	--	5	--	--	294	161	--	1	--	--	--	489
Laclede	--	0	8	--	2	80	65	--	0	--	--	--	166
Maries	16	7	19	3	28	116	182	--	38	--	--	2	433
Miller	9	1	24	20	16	322	339	10	24	--	--	1	794
Morgan	12	--	13	3	2	83	88	2	7	--	--	3	228
Phelps	4	10	91	1	4	592	481	0	80	--	--	1	1,290
Polk	1	--	9	--	0	111	86	--	15	--	--	--	360
Pulaski	--	4	15	--	2	78	62	--	10	--	--	--	190
St. Clair	1	0	16	--	1	58	25	--	3	--	--	1	137
Total	45	30	274	31	58	2,171	1,891	13	212	--	--	9	5,151
Prairie Unit													
Adair	5	2	9	1	23	59	80	--	0	--	--	1	239
Andrew	25	--	--	--	4	3	2	--	4	--	--	0	40
Atchison	3	--	--	0	0	--	1	--	--	--	--	--	8
Audrain	30	1	29	0	19	202	85	--	24	--	--	19	448
Barton	0	0	160	--	83	167	111	--	80	--	--	1	694
Bates	1	1	35	--	2	24	11	--	1	--	--	2	97
Buchanan	--	--	--	--	39	39	26	--	--	--	--	--	132
Caldwell	17	2	3	--	41	9	7	--	4	--	--	3	91
Carroll	118	5	12	--	51	42	18	--	19	--	--	19	299
Cass	0	0	28	--	1	73	68	--	27	--	--	41	244
Chariton	29	5	9	0	24	145	57	--	30	--	--	20	355
Clark	111	10	37	1	33	251	174	--	8	--	--	1	689
Clay	4	1	1	--	1	1	2	--	2	--	--	1	11
Clinton	2	0	0	--	2	3	2	--	1	--	--	0	14
Cooper	33	--	1	0	1	29	36	--	13	--	--	9	141

(Table 13 continued on next page)

Table 13.—Continued

Prairie Unit (cont.)

County												Total
Dade	1	0	--	1	--	26	14	--	3	--	1	78
Daviess	134	24	30	0	70	33	46	--	47	--	23	450
De Kalb	16	1	1	--	4	3	3	--	4	--	1	36
Gentry	58	1	1	--	5	3	5	--	4	--	2	85
Greene	--	1	7	--	0	76	38	--	6	--	1	185
Grundy	89	16	22	--	52	27	26	--	28	--	16	312
Harrison	77	14	16	--	19	21	19	--	20	--	13	233
Henry	2	0	25	--	2	46	44	--	13	--	3	152
Holt	13	--	--	--	3	2	2	--	2	--	--	24
Jasper	0	0	6	--	3	48	22	--	4	--	2	111
Johnson	12	0	7	--	4	22	22	--	23	--	2	101
Knox	15	4	16	1	47	62	56	--	4	--	1	229
Lafayette	24	1	2	--	2	8	3	--	4	--	4	50
Lawrence	--	0	44	--	0	237	124	--	21	--	0	519
Lewis	33	9	22	1	45	107	135	--	8	--	1	408
Lincoln	59	1	24	4	37	158	79	--	26	--	12	428
Linn	4	1	4	0	33	24	14	--	1	--	0	92
Livingston	72	4	9	0	29	19	16	--	15	--	4	185
Macon	5	4	15	0	15	155	72	--	4	--	3	283
Marion	2	2	6	1	3	35	30	--	3	--	1	90
Mercer	38	13	14	0	16	17	17	--	14	--	15	167
Monroe	11	3	11	0	14	160	68	--	23	--	6	314
Nodaway	40	--	0	--	4	2	1	--	4	--	1	54
Pettis	13	--	5	0	3	56	57	--	27	--	13	217
Pike	66	1	42	4	46	219	47	--	32	--	24	526
Putnam	4	--	1	0	16	14	21	--	0	--	--	64
Ralls	15	1	28	0	28	165	79	--	9	--	16	371
Randolph	33	20	52	0	38	498	328	--	69	--	28	1,124
Ray	29	2	4	--	4	8	5	--	6	--	4	67
Saline	22	1	2	0	4	16	16	--	5	--	5	92
Schuyler	4	1	7	0	48	28	42	--	0	--	--	233
Scotland	19	3	13	1	180	99	44	--	3	--	1	416
Shelby	2	2	9	1	10	120	31	--	3	--	1	186
Sullivan	3	--	1	0	16	8	26	--	3	--	1	62
Vernon	2	0	15	--	14	35	14	--	--	--	--	131
Worth	18	--	0	--	2	1	2	--	0	--	0	26
Total	1,314	156	786	15	1,139	3,608	2,248	--	655	--	322	11,600

Table 13.—Continued

| | | | | | | | Hardwoods | | | | | | |
Forest Inventory Unit and county	Cotton-wood	Elm	Hickory	Hard maple	Soft maple	Red oak group	White oak group	Sweet-gum	Syca-more	Tupelo/gum	Yellow-poplar	Other hard-woods	Total hard-woods
Riverborder Unit													
Boone	11	4	21	0	8	133	121	--	33	--	--	4	365
Callaway	1	--	9	1	5	58	74	--	14	--	--	1	178
Cape Girardeau	7	0	85	26	--	237	155	1	0	0	40	1	591
Cole	12	2	10	6	21	113	113	2	20	--	--	2	315
Dunklin	0	1	6	--	1	24	13	6	3	--	--	--	60
Franklin	13	2	32	2	19	168	162	1	24	--	--	1	444
Gasconade	83	3	20	5	32	141	205	1	42	--	--	3	549
Howard	4	1	10	0	8	61	39	--	25	--	--	5	176
Jefferson	1	1	14	1	2	101	57	0	3	--	--	1	185
Mississippi	1	--	1	--	--	--	--	--	--	--	--	--	2
Moniteau	1	--	12	3	2	85	84	2	6	--	--	1	220
Montgomery	54	--	21	4	33	105	50	--	22	--	--	12	324
New Madrid	1	6	3	--	--	7	8	12	2	--	--	37	75
Osage	42	4	20	8	49	236	304	--	45	--	--	8	744
Pemiscot	--	0	--	--	0	--	--	--	--	--	--	--	0
Perry	7	1	130	75	1	789	436	2	3	1	275	0	1,865
Scott	1	0	11	4	--	3	10	15	1	--	27	--	73
St. Charles	30	0	1	2	15	17	17	--	11	--	--	0	100
St. Louis	--	--	0	0	1	2	8	--	0	--	--	0	13
Ste. Genevieve	5	--	38	16	--	185	119	1	1	--	28	1	425
Stoddard	5	8	43	0	3	116	118	11	21	--	--	1	329
Warren	50	0	2	4	25	32	62	--	19	--	--	0	205
Total	331	32	489	157	226	2,614	2,154	53	294	1	370	78	7,240
State total	1,742	338	5,244	424	1,569	34,960	17,186	139	1,652	130	465	442	67,382

All table cells without observations are indicated by --. Table value of 0 indicates the volume rounds to less than 1 thousand cubic feet. Columns and rows may not add to their totals due to rounding.

Table 14.—Disposition of residues produced at primary wood-using mills, in thousand green tons, by Forest Inventory Unit, disposition, residue type, and softwoods and hardwoods, Missouri, 2009

Forest Inventory Unit and disposition	Total all residues		Total wood residue		Residue type					
					Wood residue				Bark	
					Coarse[a]		Fine[b]			
	Softwood	Hardwood	Softwood	Hardwood	Softwood	Hardwood	Softwood	Hardwood	Softwood	Hardwood
All Units										
Fiber products	4.0	166.2	4.0	160.4	2.2	148.5	1.8	11.8	0.0	5.8
Charcoal	13.3	503.2	11.7	415.5	6.9	268.8	4.9	146.7	1.6	87.7
Industrial fuel	8.6	150.8	7.7	134.6	3.1	53.8	4.6	80.8	0.9	16.2
Residential fuel	1.2	80.9	1.1	64.9	0.7	49.6	0.3	15.3	0.2	16.0
Miscellaneous[c]	45.3	467.5	31.8	307.2	21.1	168.6	10.7	138.6	13.6	160.3
Not used	7.0	67.5	5.1	44.8	2.7	27.0	2.4	17.7	1.9	22.8
Total	79.4	1,436.1	61.3	1,127.3	36.6	716.4	24.7	410.9	18.1	308.7
Eastern Ozark Unit										
Fiber products	3.3	69.7	3.3	69.5	2.2	62.1	1.1	7.4	0.0	0.2
Charcoal	9.5	312.5	8.4	260.2	5.0	160.7	3.4	99.5	1.1	52.3
Industrial fuel	5.0	50.7	4.2	43.8	1.6	5.8	2.6	38.0	0.8	6.9
Residential fuel	0.6	8.1	0.6	7.3	0.3	6.0	0.3	1.3	0.1	0.8
Miscellaneous[c]	26.1	167.5	17.1	104.4	10.9	68.8	6.2	35.6	9.0	63.1
Not used	4.3	31.6	3.1	19.6	1.6	8.8	1.5	10.8	1.2	12.1
Total	48.8	640.1	36.6	504.8	21.5	312.3	15.1	192.5	12.2	135.4
Southwestern Ozark Unit										
Fiber products	0.7	26.3	0.7	26.3	0.7	23.4	0.7	2.9	--	--
Charcoal	3.5	129.5	3.1	104.8	1.9	75.0	1.2	29.8	0.5	24.7
Industrial fuel	2.7	37.2	2.6	32.5	1.1	17.9	1.5	14.7	0.1	4.7
Residential fuel	0.1	18.6	0.1	16.8	0.0	6.5	0.0	10.3	0.0	1.8
Miscellaneous[c]	11.4	83.7	8.0	52.1	5.7	28.3	2.2	23.8	3.4	31.6
Not used	0.3	1.9	--	0.4	--	0.1	--	0.3	0.3	1.5
Total	18.6	297.2	14.4	232.9	8.8	151.2	5.6	81.7	4.2	64.3

Table 14.—Continued

Forest Inventory Unit and disposition	Total all residues		Residue type									
			Wood residue								Bark	
			Total wood residue		Coarse[a]		Fine[b]					
	Softwood	Hardwood	Softwood	Hardwood	Softwood	Hardwood	Softwood	Hardwood	Softwood	Hardwood		
Northwestern Ozark Unit												
Fiber products	--	3.7	--	2.6	--	2.6	--	--	--	1.1		
Charcoal	--	19.2	--	15.0	--	10.1	--	4.9	--	4.2		
Industrial fuel	0.6	2.8	0.5	2.2	0.4	1.4	0.1	0.8	0.1	0.6		
Residential fuel	0.1	8.4	0.1	6.1	0.1	5.5	--	0.6	0.0	2.3		
Miscellaneous[c]	4.1	40.3	3.5	31.4	2.3	21.0	1.3	10.4	0.6	8.9		
Not used	2.1	2.0	1.8	1.7	1.0	0.8	0.8	0.9	0.3	0.3		
Total	6.9	76.3	5.9	59.0	3.8	41.3	2.2	17.6	1.0	17.4		
Prairie Unit												
Fiber products	--	25.6	--	21.6	--	20.1	--	1.5	--	4.0		
Charcoal	--	14.4	--	13.3	--	10.2	--	3.1	--	1.2		
Industrial fuel	0.4	43.3	0.4	39.3	--	24.0	0.4	15.3	--	4.0		
Residential fuel	0.1	38.6	0.1	29.1	0.1	26.1	--	3.0	0.0	9.5		
Miscellaneous[c]	0.1	111.0	0.1	81.4	0.0	35.8	0.1	45.6	0.0	29.6		
Not used	0.0	26.8	0.0	19.3	0.0	15.1	0.0	4.3	--	7.5		
Total	0.5	259.8	0.5	204.0	0.1	131.2	0.5	72.8	0.0	55.8		
Riverborder Unit												
Fiber products	--	41.0	--	40.5	--	40.4	--	0.1	--	0.5		
Charcoal	0.2	27.5	0.2	22.2	--	12.8	0.2	9.4	--	5.3		
Industrial fuel	0.1	16.8	0.1	16.8	--	4.7	0.1	12.0	--	--		
Residential fuel	0.3	7.2	0.3	5.5	0.3	5.5	0.0	0.0	0.1	1.7		
Miscellaneous[c]	3.7	65.0	3.1	37.9	2.1	14.7	0.9	23.2	0.6	27.1		
Not used	0.3	5.2	0.2	3.8	0.1	2.3	0.1	1.5	0.1	1.4		
Total	4.6	162.6	3.8	126.7	2.5	80.4	1.3	46.3	0.8	35.9		

All table cells without observations are indicated by – . Table value of 0.0 indicates the volume rounds to less than 0.1 thousand green tons. Columns and rows may not add to their totals due to rounding.

[a] Suitable for chipping such as slabs, edgings, veneer cores, etc.
[b] Not suitable for chipping such as sawdust, veneer clippings etc.
[c] Livestock bedding, mulch, small dimension, specialty items, etc.

www.ingramcontent.com/pod-product-compliance
Lightning Source LLC
Chambersburg PA
CBHW081229280526
45787CB00006B/2582